M000222463

Cover Art: *Blodeuwedd* by Emily Brunner
Front and back cover design by Kelly Woo

Copyright 2016 Selection & editorial matter, Ninth Wave Press
Copyright 2016 Individual pieces, original contributors
All rights reserved

No part of this publication may be reproduced, stored in, or introduced into a retrieval system, or transmitted in any form, or by any means (electronic, mechanical, photocopying, recording, or otherwise) without prior permission of the publisher with the exception of reviewers who may quote brief passages in the context of their review.

Requests for permission should be directed to: info@ninthwavepress.com

Ninth Wave Press
The publishing arm of The Sisterhood of Avalon
www.ninthwavepress.com

The Sisterhood of Avalon is a fully incorporated, non-profit international Celtic Women's Mysteries Organization which seeks to balance Intuitive Wisdom with Scholastic Achievement. Among our activities, we sponsor the Avalonian Thealogical Seminary; facilitate international training intensives; host Spiritual Pilgrimages to Wales, Glastonbury and other Celtic Sacred Sites through Mythic Seeker Spiritual Pilgrimages; publish devotional anthologies and keepsake datebooks through Ninth Wave Press; and provide a variety of learning opportunities both through our local hearth groups and our online community support. Find out more about the Sisterhood online at
www.sisterhoodofavalon.org

ISBN 978-0-9789045-9-3

Dedication

To all those who have dared…
    … the Self Seekers
    … the Rule Breakers
    … the Challengers of the Status Quo

To all those who have taken a stand…
    … against violence and violation
    … against bigotry and discrimination
    … against injustice in every form

To all those who have risked everything…
    … to escape oppression
    … to live life on their own terms
    … to know what it is to be truly free

And to those who have not yet discovered the truth of who they are…
    … the truth of their power
    … the truth of their wisdom
    … the truth of their right to define themselves and their lives

        … know that you deserve safety, and love, and fulfillment
        … know that you can do it
        … know that you are not alone

May your lives be blessed with the sweetness of flowers, your days be spent in the light of your truth, and your nights be guarded by the talons of owls that you may hold fast to the power of your sovereignty.

Table of Contents

Acknowledgements

Ninth Wave Press would like to thank all of the contributors in this volume for sharing so generously their personal devotions to our Lady, Blodeuwedd. It is through your myriad collective gifts that we are able to bring this reclaimed vision of Her to the greater Goddess community.

We would also like to thank our Publications Committee for their tireless work on this very special labor of love:

- Kelly Woo, Committee Chair, for bringing her creative talents to the flawless cover design and layout work and for guiding us skillfully through the publication process.

- Maddi Jabin, for scoring the musical offerings of our contributors

- Rachael Pontillo, Margo Wolfe, Kathleen Opon, and Tiffany Lazic, for hours of meticulous proofing and copy-editing

- Kate Brunner, for publication process research, marketing planning, and assorted bits and pieces of copy

- Lori Feldmann, for getting us to the finish line with her editing prowess and attention to detail

And to all our committee members, past and present who have contributed their talents over the years to make this debut anthology a reality.

Special thanks to Jhenah Telyndru, Morgen of the Sisterhood of Avalon, for creating and sustaining the spiritual vision that originally birthed this project. It is through her unwavering commitment in Service to Goddess that Ninth Wave Press and the Sisterhood of Avalon bring you this first volume of our devotional anthology series.

.

Foreword

BY JHENAH TELYNDRU

*B*lodeuwedd.

Flower Face. Maiden of the Spring. May Bride. Betraying Wife. Night-hunting owl, reviled and hated.

Blodeuwedd. Flower Face. Keen-Eyed Hunter in the Night.

She stands along the edge of myth, her taloned form enshrouded in darkness where once she had been enrobed in flowers, basking in the warmth of the sun. Her once-honeyed voice now a raptor's screech, her words stolen from her…her tale told by others.

The story of Blodeuwedd begins with her creation from flowers for a single purpose—to wed Lleu Llaw Gyffes and circumvent the destiny lain upon him by his mother, Arianrhod. At first obedient and yielding to the expectations of others, she was the perfect wife and consort. When she came to discover her own true will, and grew to love a man of her own choosing, she was cruelly punished by the enchanter Gwydion. Cursed to dwell in darkness for all eternity, she was transformed from her beautiful aspect to inhabit the body of an ill-omened owl for her role in the betrayal of her husband. Condemned to live forever in the shadows of night, never again to see the light of day, she became scorned by all other birds and they attacked her whenever they saw her face—a face which reflected the flowers from which she had been created, the flowers from which she took her very name. Blodeuwedd. Flower Face.

Embodying the folkloric motif of the Unfaithful Wife, Blodeuwedd's centuries-old story has been used as an object lesson, her punishment a warning to any women who would dare to risk everything to change their circumstance, no matter how dire the consequences.

But, what if...?

What if there are layers of truth hidden below the surface reading of her tale, waiting between the lines on each page, calling to us from that liminal space between the letters of each word...? What if the truth about the nature of Blodeuwedd dwells in that place between what is known and what is understood? What if the true darkness of her exile has nothing to do with being condemned to an eternity of night, but rather is a measure of what remains when the sovereignty of women is withheld from them, and the stories which should empower and embolden them instead are used as tools of shame and control?

What if Blodeuwedd's transformation from Flower Maiden to Owl is not a punishment imposed upon her by her father-creator, but rather is a measure of the degree of wisdom she has obtained by discovering her true self? What if she is daring to live a life of her own choosing instead of accepting the roles placed upon her by society and fulfilling the expectations of others to her own detriment?

What if instead of the Unfaithful Wife, she is the Spring Maiden, the Flower Bride, the Goddess of Sovereignty who makes the Sacred Marriage to the King on behalf of the land, choosing the one who will rule the Light Half of the Year, as well as the one who will rule the Dark? What if she is also the Owl Goddess whose keen eyes see with wisdom through the deep void of Shadow, and whose sharp claws hold tightly to her inner truth, never letting go of all she is and all she wishes to become?

Thus understood...her story thus remembered, reclaimed, and renewed... Blodeuwedd can leave the shade of the Otherworld behind, instead dancing into the returning dawn to don her blooming mantle of rebirth. Her energy rejuvenates the Land, granting Sovereignty to those she deems worthy. Rejecting the confines created by the expectations of others, it is the choice to live her truth that causes Blodeuwedd to trade her fragile petals for a feathered cloak of her own design...to wear as she chooses.

And just as we may come to see her with new eyes, to understand the lesson of her story in a way that also informs our own path of growth, our own journey into wisdom…so too may we turn those owl eyes upon our own nature, and hear her call to us from the deepest part of our souls: "Whoooo? Whoooo? Whoooo are you?"

May we, like Blodeuwedd, discover the truth of our sovereignty…and may we, too, hold fast to what we find, no matter what others will think of us. For this is the way of growth, the way of change. The way of wisdom.

The way of the Owl Maiden. Blodeuwedd.

Jhenah Telyndru, Gwyl Mair 2016

Introduction

On the Nature of Blodeuwedd

BY JHENAH TELYNDRU

*T*here are few female characters in Welsh Mythology which present as great a moral challenge to modern readers as Blodeuwedd, who appears in the Fourth Branch of the collection of tales called *Y Mabinogi*. For many spiritual seekers that follow modern Pagan paths which draw inspiration from British Mythos, the characters in the Four Branches are honored and actively worshiped as divinities, and yet there is debate both in the academic and Neo-Pagan communities as to whether the characters in *Y Mabinogi* can be considered divinities at all, since they are not explicitly labeled as such in the text. Exploring a bit of the history of this piece of literature as well as its cultural context can help us put both the tales in general and Blodeuwedd in particular into perspective.

The earliest surviving redactions of the tales of the Four Branches date from the 13th or 14th centuries CE, far into the Christian period of Britain and Wales. The tales were preserved in two manuscripts, the *Red Book of Hergest* and the *White Book of Rhydderch*. Set down into writing during a period of political upheaval which saw Wales lose its autonomy to the Anglo-Saxons, it is believed that a nationalistic movement to preserve Welsh traditional culture in the face of these changes motivated the redaction of the Four Branches and other Welsh tales during this time; as such, it is likely the stories did not originate in this time period, but rather were captured in writing (with, perhaps, an unknown degree of authorial latitude) for the first time after possibly centuries of existing in oral tradition. We cannot say for certain how far back the stories go, nor can we pinpoint their specific places of origin with any certitude, although there is no doubt of the orality of these tales. Welsh scholar Sioned Davies points to specific sections of the text which are formulaic phrases used in recitation. Additionally, there are passages in the Four Branches whose very structure point to an older period than the accepted dating of the *Red and White Books*. For example, the *englynion*—a type of Welsh poetic verse—spoken by Gwydion in the Fourth Branch, are widely accepted to be the most ancient sections of the text, with the poetry form dating as far back as at least the ninth century CE.

These kinds of contextual clues aside, we cannot prove definitively that the stories of *Y Mabinogi* date back into pagan Celtic times, although there is plenty of symbolic subtext which suggest this might be the case, especially when compared to the myths of other Celtic peoples. Irish myth is filled with divinities, many of whom are believed to be Gaelic reflexes of Brythonic deities, or perhaps represent different tribal iterations of a common divinity set originating in the proto-Celtic mother culture, evolving distinctively over time and as a reflection of different geographic and cultural needs. Further, it is a popular theory to see Otherworldly beings such as faeries, or characters possessing supernatural abilities or exaggerated attributes—such as having enormous size or incredible strength—as demoted gods and goddesses, sometimes depicted simply as kings and queens in the text. This is a process known as "reverse euhemerization" whereby divinities are, over time, reduced in stature to become mortal heroes or historical figures. The almost casual use of magic and the easy interaction with the Otherworld found in the tales suggests a world where the fantastical was accepted and supernatural beings walked closely with humans, all the while existing outside of the medieval Christian paradigm.

Certainly it would seem odd to otherwise infuse abilities, privileges, and stature to characters which did not reflect the current cultural context of the time in which the tales were written down. For example, during the medieval period, women did not possess lordship over their own lands or autonomy over their own bodies, having to be under the legal protection of their fathers, brothers, and sons depending on their life stage and circumstance; and yet, we have female characters such as Arianrhod who are fully autonomous characters, exhibiting freedoms and authority not in keeping with medieval realities. Now it may be that these kinds of anachronisms were preserved in the text as moral cautionary tales, explaining, as myths often do, what happens when the proper order of things are circumvented, but it is indeed tempting to see through them back into a distant past where the rights and privileges of women were markedly different—and remembered.

Etymologically speaking, the names of many of the characters in *Y Mabinogi* are quite evocative, and their meanings may also point to beings of divine origin. Arianrhod, for example, means "Silver Wheel", which could point to her having once been a Moon Goddess, while Rhiannon means "Great Queen", which, along with her totemic horse symbolism, is believed to reflect her status as a Sovereignty Goddess. The names of both Ceridwen ("Holy Song/White Sow") and Branwen ("White Raven") contain the Welsh suffix "-wen" which means "shining, white, holy" and could have been a name marker to indicate a divinity; scholars believe that the -wen suffix was used in the Christian period to honor female saints. This descriptor is also seen in the name of Gwyn ap Nudd ("Light, son of Night") known from folklore as the King of the Fairies and leader of the Wild Hunt, who, on every Calan Gaeaf (Samhain), would gather the souls of those who had died during the year and bring them to the Otherworld through Glastonbury Tor.

In the Fourth Branch, there are many signs that point to the divine status of the character Blodeuwedd. Created from flowers of oak, broom, and meadowsweet, she is conjured into being through the enchantments of Math, Lord of Gwynedd, and his nephew Gwydion, both of whom are powerful magicians. She is created to be the wife of Gwydion's nephew and foster-son, Lleu, in order to circumvent the third tynged (meaning "destiny" or "fate", roughly the Welsh equivalent of the Irish geis) placed upon Lleu by his mother, Arianrhod; this tynged declared that he was forbidden to marry a woman of the race of the earth. As Lleu's manhood and future kingship depended on his taking a wife, it was critical for his uncles to secure one for him, even in the face of his mother's prohibition. The creation of Blodeuwedd, whose name means "Flower Face", out of flowers not only bypassed—or perhaps, if considered in another way, fulfilled—Arianrhod's requirement for her son. It also represented the well-established Celtic folkloric motif that required the king to make a sacred marriage with the land. This union was accomplished through the Goddess of Sovereignty or her earthly representative; how better to illustrate this than by manifesting a woman made completely from flowers —a component of the land?

We are told in the text that Blodeuwedd is named and baptized "in the manner of the day", another hint perhaps of a different religious paradigm being preserved in the stories, and was wed to Lleu that very night. After marrying Blodeuwedd, Lleu is now worthy to rule, and is set up with lands of his own by his uncle Math, underscoring the idea that she is a Sovereignty figure. Conscientious in his duties, Lleu would circumambulate his holdings, ensuring balance and lawfulness in the land. The name Lleu is sometimes given as Llew, which directly translated means "lion" in Welsh. However, when rendered as Lleu, his name means "light" and as such, he holds associations with the sun. Lleu himself is considered a Welsh reflex of the Irish god Lugh, another solar deity, and as such, Lleu's travels across his lands may represent the sun's daily path across the sky, or else the summertime, known in the various Celtic cultures as the Light Half of the Year.

It is during one of Lleu's sojourns that Gronw Pebyr, lord of Penllyn, the land neighboring Lleu's, finds himself out late hunting, pursuing a stag which has made its way on to Lleu's lands. Blodeuwedd is made aware of the neighboring lord's presence on her holdings, and decides that the laws of hospitality dictate that she invite Gronw and his hunting party for a feast and overnight accommodations. When the two of them meet, they are overcome with love for each other, and spend the night together. Gronw tries to leave the next day, but Blodeuwedd convinces him to stay with her and again they spend the night in lovemaking. The same thing happens on the third night, and then finally the next morning, Blodeuwedd tells Gronw he should depart, for her husband will be returning. They craft a plan between them to find a way whereby Lleu could be killed so that they could be together.

To the modern reader, this betrayal by Blodeuwedd seems unconscionable, but the meaning shifts if we look at these events through the eyes of the contemporary medieval audience. Unlike other female characters in the Four Branches, Blodeuwedd has no opportunity to exert any degree of autonomy, nor is she given the right of refusal of her marriage. According to the Welsh Laws, a woman could not be married against her will, and we see plenty of consent given elsewhere in Y Mabinogi. In the First Branch, Rhiannon chooses Pwyll as her husband, manipulating events to ensure that she will marry the man she has chosen; in the Third Branch, Rhiannon consents to marriage with Manawyddan at the suggestion of her son after Pwyll's death. In the Second Branch, Matholwch, the king of Ireland, asks for Branwen's hand in order to unify the two countries, and this is negotiated by her family in accordance with the Welsh laws. Blodeuwedd, however, is not shown to have any such opportunity to decline, having been created out of magic for the sole purpose of being wed to Lleu; this lack of consent may have rendered the marriage null in the eyes of the law, and as such, completely changes the character of Blodeuwedd's actions.

Consulting the medieval Welsh Laws of Women, we see that the law code provided for nine different kinds of marriage, ranked by the degree of honor each held and the amount of protection each afforded the woman in terms of property, dowry, and compensation during divorce. The most respected form of marriage is what is seen elsewhere in Y Mabinogi, illustrated by the marriages of Branwen and Rhiannon. This is called "priodas", which was a union of two people of equal rank and financial stature. In the Fourth Branch, Blodeuwedd and Gronw engaged in a "llathlud twyll" (false or secret elopement), a type of marriage called "caradas" (marriage for love), wherein a woman chose a man without the permission of her family, and slept publicly with that man for three nights in a row. While this was a legally recognized marriage, it did not carry the same respect and protection that the marriage of the type into which Rhiannon and Branwen enter.

If we consider the magical or Otherworldly elements of the narrative to be signposts for the former pagan Celtic culture, the entire love triangle of Lleu, Blodeuwedd, and Gronw—and its attendant deaths and transformations—may represent a memory of a year myth. Much like the battle at the ford between Pwyll and Hafgan in the First Branch that saw the victorious Pwyll become Pen Annwfn (Chief of the Otherworld), the back and forth defeat and victory of Lleu and Gronw for the hand of the Flower Bride may be another reiteration of this mythic motif. The alternating casting of the spear occurs on the banks of a river, a liminal place symbolizing the presence of the Otherworld, indicating that the action takes place between the worlds, straddling them as with the great festivals of Calan Gaeaf and Calan Mai—gateways between the dark and light halves of the year. Indeed, even the requirements for Lleu's destruction exhibit the in-between motif of the Otherworld:

> "'I cannot be killed indoors,' [Lleu] said, 'nor out of doors; I cannot be killed on horseback nor on foot.'
>
> 'Well,' [Blodeuwedd] said, "how can you be killed?'
>
> 'I will tell you,' he said. 'By making a bath for me on a riverbank, and constructing an arched roof above the tub, and then thatching that well and watertight. And by bringing a billy-goat,' he said, 'and standing it beside the tub; and I place one foot on the back of the billy-goat and the other on the edge of the tub. Whoever should strike me in that position would bring about my death'" (Davies 2007, 60)

In addition to these conditions, Lleu must also be struck with a spear created only during Sunday mass in order to be killed. That the spear must be created during sacred time is significant, as is its obvious phallic symbolism as the object through which Blodeuwedd, and by extension sovereignty and the land, can be obtained.

Ultimately, Gwydion heals Lleu who, instead of dying at the spear point of Gronw is transformed into a wounded eagle, and Blodeuwedd is punished by being transformed into an owl by her creator. Perhaps then, this is a mythic memory, strong enough to make its way into the written record. Notably, the eagle and the oak tree are ancient symbols of the Celtic sky god Taranis who is conflated with Jupiter in Romano-Celtic iconography, while the owl is an ancient goddess totem—one usually associated with wisdom. In the contemporary medieval Welsh tale *Culhwch and Olwen*, both the owl and the eagle are counted among the Oldest Animals in a segment of the story which may be a reflection of some ancient British totemic tribal system.

At the end of the Fourth Branch, the restored Lleu challenges Gronw in a bid to reclaim his lands. They meet again on the banks of the same river where Gronw wounded Lleu, and Lleu demands justice by having the opportunity to cast a spear at Gronw in the same fashion one was cast at him. Gronw asks permission to hold a stone between himself and Lleu, since the whole matter occurred over a woman, and although Lleu agrees, it does Gronw no good; Lleu's spear pierces the stone and kills Gronw there on the banks of the river—sending him to the Otherworld. The two faces of Blodeuwedd underscore this polarity myth. She is an owl when she is mated with the Otherworldly Champion, and a Flower Bride when wed to the Solar Hero.

If this is indeed an onomastic reenactment of the year myth, representing the endless struggle between light and dark or summer and winter, it is significant that Blodeuwedd is the pivot around which the balance shifts. This may be an indication of her former status as a representative of the Goddess of the land—indeed, she is literally made of nature—and as an extension, she is the Goddess of Sovereignty. As such, she has the right to choose her mate—no matter what Gwydion may contrive—and who she chooses becomes king. This may be why she could not simply have run away with Gronw—only one king can reign at a time. Further, the Fourth Branch's inclusion of the onomastic story of the hole in the stone called Llech Ronw (the Stone of Gronw) is a further reiteration of the feminine principle—the yonic hole through which kingship is obtained—or, in this case, reasserted.

Whether she is simply a legendary figure from medieval Welsh lore, or is in truth a Sovereignty Goddess once worshiped in Celtic Britain, there is no doubt that Blodeuwedd is celebrated and honored in modern times as a divinity in her own right. After dwelling for centuries in darkness, flying on owl wings along the liminal boundary that straddles superstition and sacred symbol... this world and the Otherworld...archetype and Divinity...the essence of all that is Blodeuwedd is venturing once more into the light of consciousness. Simultaneously Flower Bride and Owl of Wisdom, Unfaithful Wife and Lady of Sovereignty, this complex figure holds many lessons for those who seek to know her, and through her, learn to shed the fragile petals of illusion wrought by the expectations of others, in order to birth the authentic Self that is able to see Truth with owl-wise eyes.

As part of the movement to understand the deeper significance which underscores her myth found in the Fourth Branch of *Y Mabinogi*, here then is a collection of essays and meditations; poetry and songs; drawings and photographs; scholarly research and experiential encounters, which explore the nature of Blodeuwedd in all of her facets—remembering her mythos, reclaiming her Divine Status, and renewing her role as an initiatory Goddess who empowers us to be free.

I Am Free

Alicia Grosso

Words and Music by Alicia Grosso © 2008. All rights reserved.

Invocation to Blodeuwedd

BY JHENAH TELYNDRU

Holy Blodeuwedd, Lady of Nine Flowers,
Fill me with your blessings of renewal and the joy of empowered flight.
Flower Faced One,
Teach me the power of my choices so that I may embrace my authentic self,
even in the face of others' expectations.
Keen-eyed Hunter in the Night,
Help me to see past the illusion-shrouded darkness
so that my eyes may stay focused on that which is the essence of my being,
my sharp talons never losing their grip upon the path of Truth.

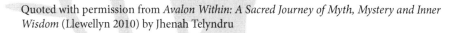

Quoted with permission from *Avalon Within: A Sacred Journey of Myth, Mystery and Inner Wisdom* (Llewellyn 2010) by Jhenah Telyndru

The Tale of Blodeuwedd

An Excerpt from the Fourth Branch of the Mabinogi, Math the Son of Mathonwy

TRANSLATED BY LADY CHARLOTTE GUEST, 1877
WITH AN INTRODUCTION BY JHENAH TELYNDRU

*M*ath ap Mathonwy is the lord of Gwynedd in Wales. A powerful magician, the tale explains that nevertheless he "could not exist unless his feet were in the lap of a maiden, except only when he was prevented by the tumult of war." His footholder was a woman named Goewin, and one of his nephews, Gilvaethwy, became sick with his love for her. Gilvaethwy's brother, Gwydion, was also a magician, and he conspired to help his brother by catalyzing a war between Math and Pryderi ap Pwyll, lord of South Wales. While Math was at war, Gilvaethwy raped Goewin. Furious upon his return, Math married Goewin, and punished his nephews by changing them into various beasts who would bear each other children, a different animal each year of their three year punishment. When Gwydion and Gilvaethwy are restored, Math asks Gwydion's assistance to find him a new footholder; his nephew recommends his sister, Arianrhod. She is brought to court and is asked if she is a maiden. She replies "I know not, lord, other than that I am." Math bids her prove her virginity by stepping over his magic wand, and upon doing so, two things drop from her body: a fully grown baby who crawls away into the sea, becoming Dylan of the Waves, and a small thing that Gwydion snatches up and hides away in a chest at the foot of his bed. Arianrhod, dishonored, runs from the court. Gwydion later finds that the small thing in his chest has grown to become a fully-formed baby, who grows more quickly than a regular child. He brings the boy to Arianrhod's court, but she becomes angry at this reminder of her dishonor, and lays a curse upon him, "he shall never have a name until he receives one from me." Through his shape changing magic, Gwydion tricks Arianrhod into naming the boy Llew Llaw Gyffes. She *then curses the boy to bear no arms until she herself arms him, and likewise through magic, Gwydion tricks her to do so yet again. Enraged, Arianrhod lays down one final curse, and this is where the story of Blodeuwedd begins.*

"By Heaven," said Arianrod, "thou art a wicked man. Many a youth might have lost his life through the uproar thou hast caused in this Cantrev to-day. Now will I lay a destiny upon this youth," she said, "that he shall never have a wife of the race that now inhabits this earth." "Verily," said he, "thou wast ever a malicious woman, and no one ought to support thee. A wife shall he have notwithstanding."

They went thereupon unto Math the son of Mathonwy, and complained unto him most bitterly of Arianrod. Gwydion showed him also how he had procured arms for the youth. "Well," said Math, "we will seek, I and thou, by charms and illusion, to form a wife for him out of flowers. He has now come to man's stature, and he is the comeliest youth that was ever beheld." So they took the blossoms of the oak, and the blossoms of the broom, and the blossoms of the meadow-sweet, and produced from them a maiden, the fairest and most graceful that man ever saw. And they baptized her, and gave her the name of Blodeuwedd.

After she had become his bride, and they had feasted, said Gwydion, "It is not easy for a man to maintain himself without possessions." "Of a truth," said Math, "I will give the young man the best Cantrev to hold." "Lord," said he, "what Cantrev is that?" "The Cantrev of Dinodig," he answered. Now it is called at this day Eivionydd and Ardudwy. And the place in the Cantrev where he dwelt, was a palace of his in a spot called Mur y Castell, on the confines of Ardudwy. There dwelt he and reigned, and both he and his sway were beloved by all.

One day he went forth to Caer Dathyl, to visit Math the son of Mathonwy. And on the day that he set out for Caer Dathyl, Blodeuwedd walked in the Court. And she heard the sound of a horn. And after the sound of the horn, behold a tired stag went by, with dogs and huntsmen following it. And after the dogs and the huntsmen there came a crowd of men on foot. "Send a youth," said she, "to ask who yonder host may be." So a youth went, and inquired who they were. "Gronw Pebyr is this, the lord of Penllyn," said they. And thus the youth told her.

Gronw Pebyr pursued the stag, and by the river Cynvael he overtook the stag and killed it. And what with flaying the stag and baiting his dogs, he was there until the night began to close in upon him. And as the day departed and the night drew near, he came to the gate of the Court. "Verily," said Blodeuwedd, "the Chieftain will speak ill of us if we let him at this hour depart to another land without inviting him in." "Yes, truly, lady," said they, "it will be most fitting to invite him."

Then went messengers to meet him and bid him in. And he accepted her bidding gladly, and came to the Court, and Blodeuwedd went to meet him, and greeted him, and bade him welcome. "Lady," said he, "Heaven repay thee thy kindness."

When they had disaccoutred themselves, they went to sit down. And Blodeuwedd looked upon him, and from the moment that she looked on him she became filled with his love. And he gazed on her, and the same thought came unto him as unto her, so that he could not conceal from her that he loved her, but he declared unto her that he did so. Thereupon she was very joyful. And all their discourse that night was concerning the affection and love which they felt one for the other, and which in no longer space than one evening had arisen. And that evening passed they in each other's company.

The next day he sought to depart. But she said, "I pray thee go not from me to-day." And that night he tarried also. And that night they consulted by what means they might always be together. "There is none other counsel," said he, "but that thou strive to learn from Llew Llaw Gyffes in what manner he will meet his death. And this must thou do under the semblance of solicitude concerning him."

The next day Gronw sought to depart. "Verily," said she, "I will counsel thee not to go from me to-day." "At thy instance will I not go," said he, "albeit, I must say, there is danger that the chief who owns the palace may return home." "To-morrow," answered she, "will I indeed permit thee to go forth."

The next day he sought to go, and she hindered him not. "Be mindful," said Gronw, "of what I have said unto thee, and converse with him fully, and that under the guise of the dalliance of love, and find out by what means he may come to his death."

That night Llew Llaw Gyffes returned to his home. And the day they spent in discourse, and minstrelsy, and feasting. And at night they went to rest, and he spoke to Blodeuwedd once, and he spoke to her a second time. But, for all this, he could not get from her one word. "What aileth thee?" said he, "art thou well?" "I was thinking," said she, "of that which thou didst never think of concerning me; for I was sorrowful as to thy death, lest thou shouldst go sooner than I." "Heaven reward thy care for me," said he, "but until Heaven take me I shall not easily be slain" "For the sake of Heaven, and for mine, show me how thou mightest be slain. My memory in guarding is better than thine." "I will tell thee gladly," said he. "Not easily can I be slain, except by a wound. And the spear wherewith I am struck must be a year in the forming. And nothing must be done towards it except during the sacrifice on Sundays." "Is this certain?" asked she. "It is in truth," he answered. "And I cannot be slain within a house, nor without. I cannot be slain on horseback nor on foot." "Verily," said she, "in what manner then canst thou be slain?" "I will tell thee," said he. "By making a bath for me by the side of a river, and by putting a roof over the cauldron, and thatching it well and tightly, and bringing a buck, and putting it beside the cauldron. Then if I place one foot on the buck's back, and the other on the edge of the cauldron, whosoever strikes me thus will cause my death." "Well," said she, "I thank Heaven that it will be easy to avoid this."

No sooner had she held this discourse than she sent to Gronw Pebyr. Gronw toiled at making the spear, and that day twelvemonth it was ready. And that very day he caused her to be informed thereof.

"Lord," said Blodeuwedd unto Llew, "I have been thinking how it is possible that what thou didst tell me formerly can be true; wilt thou show me in what manner thou couldst stand at once upon the edge of a cauldron and upon a buck, if I prepare the bath for thee?" "I will show thee," said he.

Then she sent unto Gronw, and bade him be in ambush on the hill which is now called Bryn Kyvergyr, on the bank of the river Cynvael. She caused also to be collected all the goats that were in the Cantrev, and had them brought to the other side of the river, opposite Bryn Kyvergyr.

And the next day she spoke thus. "Lord," said she, "I have caused the roof and the bath to be prepared, and lo! they are ready." "Well," said Llew, "we will go gladly to look at them."

The day after they came and looked at the bath. "Wilt thou go into the bath, lord?" said she. "Willingly will I go in," he answered. So into the bath he went, and he anointed himself. "Lord," said she, "behold the animals which thou didst speak of as being called bucks." "Well," said he, "cause one of them to be caught and brought here." And the buck was brought. Then Llew rose out of the bath, and put on his trowsers, and he placed one foot on the edge of the bath and the other on the buck's back.

Thereupon Gronw rose up from the hill which is called Bryn Kyvergyr, and he rested on one knee, and flung the poisoned dart and struck him on the side, so that the shaft started out, but the head of the dart remained in. Then he flew up in the form of an eagle and gave a fearful scream. And thenceforth was he no more seen.

As soon as he departed Gronw and Blodeuwedd went together unto the palace that night. And the next day Gronw arose and took possession of Ardudwy. And after he had overcome the land, he ruled over it, so that Ardudwy and Penllyn were both under his sway.

Then these tidings reached Math the son of Mathonwy. And heaviness and grief came upon Math, and much more upon Gwydion than upon him. "Lord," said Gwydion, "I shall never rest until I have tidings of my nephew." "Verily," said Math, "may Heaven be thy strength." Then Gwydion set forth and began to go forward. And he went through Gwynedd and Powys to the confines. And when he had done so, he went into Arvon, and came to the house of a vassal, in Maenawr Penardd. And he alighted at the house, and stayed there that night. The man of the house and his house-hold came in, and last of all came there the swineherd. Said the man of the house to the swineherd, "Well, youth, hath thy sow come in to-night?" "She hath," said he, "and is this instant returned to the pigs." "Where doth this sow go to?" said Gwydion. "Every day, when the sty is opened, she goeth forth and none can catch sight of her, neither is it known whither she goeth more than if she sank into the earth." "Wilt thou grant unto me," said Gwydion, "not to open the sty until I am beside the sty with thee?" "This will I do, right gladly," he answered.

That night they went to rest; and as soon as the swineherd saw the light of day, he awoke Gwydion. And Gwydion arose and dressed himself, and went with the swineherd, and stood beside the sty. Then the swineherd opened the sty. And as soon as he opened it, behold she leaped forth, and set off with great speed. And Gwydion followed her, and she went against the course of a river, and made for a brook, which is now called Nant y Llew. And there she halted and began feeding. And Gwydion came under the tree, and looked what it might be that the sow was feeding on. And he saw that she was eating putrid flesh and vermin. Then looked he up to the top of the tree, and as he looked he beheld on the top of the tree an eagle, and when the eagle shook itself, there fell vermin and putrid flesh from off it, and these the sow devoured. And it seemed to him that the eagle was Llew. And he sang an Englyn:—

> "Oak that grows between the two banks;
> Darkened is the sky and hill!
> Shall I not tell him by his wounds,
> That this is Llew?"

24

Upon this the eagle came down until he reached the centre of the tree. And Gwydion sang another Englyn:—

"Oak that grows in upland ground,
Is it not wetted by the rain? Has it not been drenched
By nine score tempests?
It bears in its branches Llew Llaw Gyffes!"

Then the eagle came down until he was on the lowest branch of the tree, and thereupon this Englyn did Gwydion sing:—

"Oak that grows beneath the steep;
Stately and majestic is its aspect!
Shall I not speak it?
That Llew will come to my lap?"

And the eagle came down upon Gwydion's knee. And Gwydion struck him with his magic wand, so that he returned to his own form. No one ever saw a more piteous sight, for he was nothing but skin and bone.

Then he went unto Caer Dathyl, and there were brought unto him good physicians that were in Gwynedd, and before the end of the year he was quite healed.

"Lord," said he unto Math the son of Mathonwy, "it is full time now that I have retribution of him by whom I have suffered all this woe." "Truly," said Math, "he will never be able to maintain himself in the possession of that which is thy right." "Well," said Llew, "the sooner I have my right, the better shall I be pleased."

Then they called together the whole of Gwynedd, and set forth to Ardudwy. And Gwydion went on before and proceeded to Mur y Castell. And when Blodeuwedd heard that he was coming, she took her maidens with her, and fled to the mountain. And they passed through the river Cynvael, and went towards a court that there was upon the mountain, and through fear they could not proceed except with their faces looking backwards, so that unawares they fell into the lake. And they were all drowned except Blodeuwedd herself, and her Gwydion overtook. And he said unto her, "I will not slay thee, but I will do unto thee worse than that. For I will turn thee into a bird; and because of the shame thou hast done unto Llew Llaw Gyffes, thou shalt never show thy face in the light of day henceforth; and that through fear of all the other birds. For it shall be their nature to attack thee, and to chase thee from wheresoever they may find thee. And thou shalt not lose thy name, but shalt be always called

Blodeuwedd." Now Blodeuwedd is an owl in the language of this present time, and for this reason is the owl hateful unto all birds. And even now the owl is called Blodeuwedd.

Then Gronw Pebyr withdrew unto Penllyn, and he dispatched thence an embassy. And the messengers he sent asked Llew Llaw Gyffes if he would take land, or domain, or gold, or silver, for the injury he had received. "I will not, by my confession to Heaven," said he. "Behold this is the least that I will accept from him; that he come to the spot where I was when he wounded me with the dart, and that I stand where he did, and that with a dart I take my aim at him. And this is the very least that I will accept."

And this was told unto Gronw Pebyr. "Verily," said he, "is it needful for me to do thus? My faithful warriors, and my household, and my foster-brothers, is there not one among you who will stand the blow in my stead?" "There is not, verily," answered they. And because of their refusal to suffer one stroke for their lord, they are called the third disloyal tribe even unto this day. "Well," said he, "I will meet it."

Then they two went forth to the banks of the river Cynvael, and Gronw stood in the place where Llew Llaw Gyffes was when he struck him, and Llew in the place where Gronw was. Then said Gronw Pebyr unto Llew, "Since it was through the wiles of a woman that I did unto thee as I have done, I adjure thee by Heaven to let me place between me and the blow, the slab thou seest yonder on the river's bank." "Verily," said Llew, "I will not refuse thee this." "Ah," said he, "may Heaven reward thee." So Gronw took the slab and placed it between him and the blow.

Then Llew flung the dart at him, and it pierced the slab and went through Gronw likewise, so that it pierced through his back. And thus was Gronw Pebyr slain. And there is still the slab on the bank of the river Cynvael, in Ardudwy, having the hole through it. And therefore is it even now called Llech Gronw.

A second time did Llew Llaw Gyffes take possession of the land, and prosperously did he govern it. And, as the story relates, he was lord after this over Gwynedd. And thus ends this portion of the Mabinogi.

Retrieved from http://www.sacred-texts.com/neu/celt/mab/mab26.htm

Llech Ronw (Stone of Gronw)
This holed stone was found on the banks of the Afon Cynfael in 1934, just as described in the Fourth Branch. It was set upright along the banks of the Afon Bryn Saeth, a tributary of the Cynfael, where it can be seen to this day.

PHOTO CREDIT: JHENAH TELYNDRU

Morning Prayer to Blodeuwedd

BY JULIE BOND

O Blodeuwedd,
Maid of flowers,
The Oak, the Broom, and the Meadowsweet;
Lady called forth by Math and Gwydion,
I greet you this day.
In the summer fields the Meadowsweet blooms;
Sweet flowers of blessing and change.
O Blodeuwedd, the maid changed into the bird,
Bring me wisdom in all my transitions.
O Blodeuwedd, Flower-Face,
O Lady who made your own choice;
As blossoms garland the land
and all Nature blooms forth,
I honour you this day and this Spring.

Song for the May Queen

Words by Seren

Music by Maddi Jabin

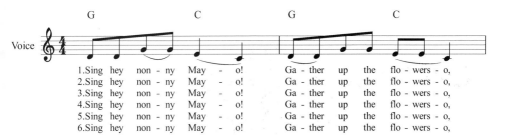

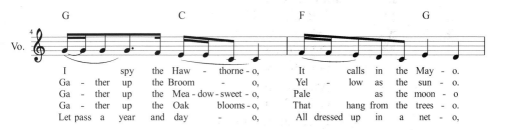

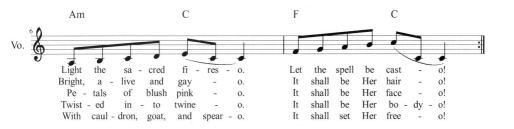

Words and Music © 2015. All rights reserved.

Emergence

BY NIMUE

I'd like to sing a song
by a friend I've never met;
Tori Amos calls out to me
from her piano bench.
I never realized
how tight I was holding on;
Thankfully Blodeuwedd
isn't prone to bruisin'.
No cotton candy clouds,
No thunderous applause,
Just Blodeuwedd and I
starin' at the walls.

Emergence 2015

WISE OWL

by Laura Bell

Reclaiming Blodeuwedd:

Seasonal Sovereignty in the Fourth Branch of *Y Mabinogi*

BY JHENAH TELYNDRU

*T*he Fourth Branch of *Y Mabinogi* is imbued with layers of symbolism which may have held deeper meaning for its medieval Welsh audience than is immediately apparent to modern readers. Redacted at a time when traditional tales were being transmitted from orality into writing, the present-day study of these stories recognizes brief textual references to other lore which likely was clearly understood by their contemporary audiences, but which leave us with only maddening glimpses into what may have been a more expansive corpus of story tradition.

One possible way to glean some additional meaning is to conduct close readings of *Y Mabinogi* and contemporary tales in order to discern patterns of symbolism and identify recurring folkloric motifs. While it is possible to recognize mythic themes in the Fourth Branch which can be classified as international folk motifs, they cannot give us a clear picture about questions of origins of the tale, nor enable us to fully understand how the exchange of ideas with other countries impacted the growth and evolution of Welsh literary tradition, as Wales increasingly participated in cultural exchange with the rest of Europe.

Several international folk motifs—including the Wild Hunt, Faithless Queen Aids Lover to Dispossess King, Hero Killed by Magical Object—are present in the Fourth Branch, as are echoes of mythemes found in Classical and Ancient Near Eastern stories, such as succession of kingship obtained by combat (*Rex nemorisis*), the life cycle of the year spirit (*eniautos daimon*) and the pervasiveness of the *hieros gamos*, or sacred marriage. The Sovereignty motif is particularly common in medieval literature, although the characteristics and purpose of Sovereignty shifts over time and with each individual culture.

The figure of Sovereignty, a woman who confers kingship and the right to rule over the land, can be found in various forms in medieval legends from Ireland and Wales, as well as in later English and French Arthurian tales. Parker identifies two types of Sovereignty: aperiodic, which is dependent on right rulership, and periodic, which he calls a "Near Eastern" type, and which sees kingship change seasonally or annually. Although most of the medieval Sovereignty legends fall into the aperiodic category, and is the type of Sovereignty which is the most discussed, the periodic type is also present, albeit implicitly, in all three general literary iterations discussed here: Irish, Welsh, and Arthurian tales from England and France.

The most recognized form of the Sovereignty motif is found in Irish literature where the female representative of the land—perhaps a goddess, otherworldly woman, or tutelary figure—tests a potential ruler and grants him kingship through sexual relations. This marriage to the land sees the usually ugly hag-like figure of Sovereignty transformed into a beautiful maiden, and she remains so for as long as the king is a righteous ruler. When he is not in right relationship with the land and his subjects, the resulting imbalance causes the land to become infertile and Sovereignty becomes a hag once more until a worthy replacement for the king is found and crowned.

In Arthurian legend, Sovereignty shifts from the political to the personal. Instead of the loathly lady granting the right to rule to a king, she instead seeks personal sovereignty from her tested mate—that is, she seeks the ability to choose and have agency over her life; when she gets it, she is transformed into a beautiful woman. Rulership over the land is sometimes included subtextually in these tales, as seen in the *The Weddynge of Sir Gawen and Dame Ragnall*, but it does not appear to be the focus of the story.

Welsh iterations of the Sovereignty motif in some instances appear to bridge the changes in the nature of Sovereignty between the Irish and Arthurian tales; Sovereignty figures are present but their roles are increasingly subtextual. We can identify them by their function or associated symbolism as they are not directly named as Sovereignty as seen in the Irish material, but we also see a precedent for the vessel of Sovereignty becoming a literal object, as in the quest for the chieftain's cauldron in *Preiddeu Annwn* as well as the cauldron of rebirth found in the Second Branch. This regenerative power is important because it carries echoes of the motif as we see it in the Irish tales, in that the state of the land depends upon the righteousness of the king, as well as presaging the Wasteland aspects of the Arthurian grail traditions. The holdings of the wounded Fisher King is a Wasteland because the king is not whole, and it is the cup or grail which will restore both king and land.

Symbols of sovereignty and kingship, both in totemic forms—especially involving horses, stags, and wrens—and in cult objects which suggest feminine form and function—like the cauldron, cup, and grail—are attested to both in legend and the archaeological record. Sovereignty serves as the threshold through which a change in status can occur; she is a bridge that connects two opposing states of being by being empowered to grant the right for the king to rule, as well as having the ability to rescind that right. When the king is united to the land by mating with Sovereignty, the status of the land is a reflection of his rulership: it thrives when he is a righteous leader and is physically whole, and it declines in response to any violation of right leadership or in the presence of any physical failings in the health of the king.

This change in status of the land, shifting in turn from fertile to fallow, can also be observed as part of the seasonal round, moving from summer to winter and back again. Concern for the turning of the seasons is a feature of any agrarian society, and it appears to play an important role in folk practice and lore in Wales, England, and Ireland. Seasonal festivals are especially keyed into the transitional periods between summer and winter, as well as that liminal threshold that moves time from one year to the next. The interplay between summer and winter has its analogues in the dualities of light and darkness, this world and the Otherworld, order and chaos, abundance and the Wasteland, and is a common motif found in many medieval tales.

The concept of "Seasonal Sovereignty" is most clearly revealed by using a structuralist analysis of these tales, especially as it concerns the primary organizing principle of the tension between binary oppositions. Levi-Strauss, a foremost structuralist, believed that all cultural products—which includes myths, symbols, folk tales, kinship organizations, and folklore—reflected this dualistic structure. To consider Seasonal Sovereignty as a motif, we must first examine the ways in which this duality expresses itself; we see a fundamental pattern arise where the polarities of darkness and light repeat themselves over and over again, in myth, seasonal folk practices, folklore, and even calendrics. In literary context, there is an emphasis on differentiating this world and the Otherworld, while drawing attention to the threshold places that facilitate the transition from one state to another. We see this boundary manifest as fords and rivers between territories (the Otherworld and this world), as transitional times of day (sunset and sunrise), as feast days which mark the shift between seasons (1st November and 1st May), and annual battles that happen every year and a day, with that additional day perhaps representing a time outside of time.

In the same way that a would-be-king seeks Sovereignty over the land, so do the seasons seek sovereignty over the year in their turn; as the impact on the fecundity of the land is the same, perhaps these dualistic struggles can be said to hold common resonances as they fulfil similar functions. When it comes to Seasonal Sovereignty, therefore, we see the duality express itself in the romantic rivals in the love triangle which characterizes this interplay; one rival exhibits characteristics of the Solar Hero motif, and the other holds correspondence with the Otherworldly Champion archetype. The rivals battle each other at points of liminality—either in threshold places or at boundary times or both —and they do so seeking the hand of the maiden who represents Sovereignty. This rivalry differs from the aperiodic Sovereignty motif because it features reversals in status between the two suitors, with their fates often mirror images of each other; one falls from prominence as the other rises, usually occurring at appointed times and in transition places. The representative of Sovereignty favours each champion in turn, and in the mould of the classic sovereignty figures, not only serves to test the rivals but often is an active participant in the other's fall. In the context of this seasonal allegory, therefore, the Sovereignty figure acts as the pivot around which the year turns, granting her favour to one suitor then the other in succession. The symmetry of the reversals suggest something deeper is going on.

In the Fourth Branch, this proposed motif is expressed in the love triangle between Lleu, Gronw, and Blodeuwedd. While the triad is traditionally identified with the Faithless Queen motif, exploring the subtextual patterns allows a different dynamic to become visible, thereby recasting the actions and motivations of all of the players—Blodeuwedd, most especially. Without this concept of the seasons taking sovereign rulership over the year as the underlying motif of this triangle, and those found in similar tales elsewhere in Welsh, Irish, and Arthurian lore, we cannot see Blodeuwedd as anything but a betraying wife, deserving of her ultimate punishments. Restoring her character's status to that of a Sovereignty figure by virtue of all of the traits they have in common allows her to be viewed in a more sympathetic light. Like other representatives of Sovereignty, Blodeuwedd has a powerful connection to the land, confers kingship, is quested after, is involved in granting and repealing Sovereignty, and changes form to reflect the status of rulership—albeit, in her case, mirroring her chosen mate: she is the Flower Bride when wed to the Solar Hero, and the Owl when paired with the Otherworldly Champion.

That we see similar seasonal dynamics at play in other love triangles found in medieval Welsh, Irish, and Arthurian tales—especially those which do not have an overt Sovereignty figure present in the narrative—suggests that the concept of Seasonal Sovereignty, which both underscored the inherent drama of romantic rivalries and served as a subtextual allegory for the switching dualities of the dark and light halves of the year, should be considered an international folk motif in its own right. Doing so permits modern readers to gain greater insight into some of the potential motivations of characters in the tales of this time period, while also shedding light on some of the cultural forms and concerns of the tales' contemporary audiences.

Lady of Sovereignty

There are several archetypal parameters which define the personification and function of Sovereignty: she is a representative of the land, often a tutelary deity or spirit; she presents challenges to the would-be king, determining his worth and initiating sexual contact; she enters into a *hieros gamos* or sacred marriage with a kingly candidate, sealing the fortunes of the land to the health and actions of the man she has, through this act, made king; she has the power to grant, and rescind if circumstances require, sovereignty over the land; and she has the ability to change shape, often as a reflection of the status of the land in relationship to the righteous king. Comparing Blodeuwedd to these common traits of the representative of Sovereignty is instructive and perhaps illuminating as to her true nature. Indeed, although the presence of possible Sovereignty figures in the Four Branches in general, and in the Fourth Branch in particular, is subtextual, it is clear that Blodeuwedd presents with many of Sovereignty's characteristics.

Blodeuwedd as Representative of the Land

In all of the many ways that Sovereignty presents herself throughout time and across cultures, perhaps there is no example of a Sovereignty figure as clearly connected to the land as Blodeuwedd. She is literally conjured by the magic of Math and Gwydion from the flowers of oak, broom, and meadowsweet to be Lleu's wife. Her very creation circumvented the *tynged* laid upon Lleu by his mother that "he will never have a wife from the race that is on this earth at present".[1] Given the specific parameters of this third and final destiny, perhaps it was Aranrhod's intention from the start that her son Lleu make a sacred marriage with the land, thus further reinforcing Aranrhod's role as an initiatory figure, assisting her son in obtaining his manhood and kingship through meeting the challenges she sets before him.

---

[1] S. Davies, *The Mabinogion* (New York: Oxford University Press, 2007), p. 58

That Blodeuwedd is created from flowers firmly ties her into the Flower Bride motif that connects her to other Sovereignty figures at the heart of a contest of champions, including Blaithnat and Gwenhwyfar. As the reproductive organs of a plant, flowers confer sexual beauty as well as fertility—two very attractive characteristics in a wife. That flowers are fragile and eventually fade is also telling, for they represent a yielding nature as well as a sense of impermanence. Why would Math and Gwydion not have created a wife for Lleu out of sturdier stuff? Surely an entire tree, for example, would have made for a less inconstant companion—unless weakness or seasonality was the intent.

The specific flowers chosen to create Blodeuwedd are significant enough for the redactor to mention in the text, and so perhaps they themselves transmitted information about Blodeuwedd's nature to the Fourth Branch's contemporary audience. The oak is a tree closely associated with the Solar Hero in many cultures, and indeed, it is this very tree which houses the wounded Lleu when he is in eagle-form (yet another solar association) later on in the tale. The broom is used as a descriptor for Olwen's yellow hair in *Culhwch ac Olwen*,[2] and while it may be mentioned to likewise allude to Blodeuwedd's hair colour, it is also a herb used in the *materia medica* of the Physicians of Myddfai to cool fevers.[3] Broom was used to cleanse the house on May Day, and was often included in bride's bouquets,[4] as was meadowsweet which is also known by the name "bridewort." Interestingly, meadowsweet has also been used as a funerary herb[5] and perhaps its presence here presages the role Blodeuwedd will play in Lleu's "death."

Blodeuwedd as Challenger of the Would-be King

In the text, it is Aranrhod, not Blodeuwedd, who puts seemingly insurmountable challenges before Lleu, all of which need to be overcome before he is able to rule. Blodeuwedd is, herself, brought into being in order to satisfy the final destiny lain upon Lleu, and in many ways, plays a very passive role in Lleu's coming into power. She is a prize, a woman created to be the perfect wife: beautiful and compliant. She is created to play a role, and unlike the other marriages we see in the Four Branches, she is not shown to give consent, nor does she have family to negotiate the marriage on her behalf. Gwydion is her

---

[2] R. Bromwich and D. Simon Evans, *Culhwch and Olwen: An Edition and Study of the Oldest Arthurian Tale*, eds. (Cardiff: University of Wales Press, 1992), p. 116

[3] *The Physicians of Myddfai*, translated by John Pughe, (Felinfach: Llanerch Publishers, 1993). p. 41

[4] J. Lawton, *Flowers and Fables: A Welsh Herbal* (Bridgend: Seren Books, 2006), p. 32

[5] Ibid., p. 134

creator, and perhaps sees himself as her father, or at least, her owner, and so of course she will play the part she was created to fill. Once again, it seems, Gwydion subverts a woman's right.

If she is passive in her connection with Lleu, Blodeuwedd is certainly acting with personal agency when it comes to Gronw, the neighbouring lord from Penllyn. She gives him hospitality as would be expected, but when the two fall in love, she boldly asks him to remain with her for three nights; although he asks each night for permission to leave, she refuses. Although this is not made explicit in the text, it may be that the medieval audience would have recognized this to be one of the legal unions provided for by Welsh Law:

> Whoever sleeps with a woman for three nights from the time when the fire is covered up until it is uncovered the next day, and wishes to repudiate her, let him pay her a bullock worth twenty pence and another worth thirty and another worth sixty. And if he takes her to house and holding, and she is with him until the end of the seven years, he shares with her as with a woman who had givers.[6]

Further, according to the Welsh Laws "…a woman must be a free consenting party to her marriage and could not be disposed of against her will…there was no selling of a woman in marriage."[7] If Blodeuwedd's lack of consent in marrying Lleu rendered *that* union illegal, then perhaps this signifies that she made a true and legal union with Gronw.

If that is the case, why then wouldn't Blodeuwedd have simply run off with Gronw, or else if this was a straightforward matter of adultery, why wouldn't the lovers just keep their tryst secret? Davies opines:

> "…committing adultery was a symbolic act in Blodeuwedd's eyes. The important thing was to rebel against patriarchal and matrimonial authority, to run away from her creator (Gwydion) and leave her owner (Lleu). And the way to cause the greatest pain to Lleu was by committing adultery. Gronw and Blodeuwedd could have kept their love secret, but by attempting to kill Lleu, the rebellion was complete… this is no ordinary adultery but rather a wife who wishes to control her own personality and freedom to use her intellect and emotion as she chooses."[8]

---

[6] J. Cartwright, *Feminine Sanctity and Spirituality in Medieval Wales* (Cardiff: University of Wales Press, 2008), p. 169

[7] T.P. Ellis, "Legal references, terms and conceptions in the Mabinogion", Y Cymmrodor 39 (1928), 86- 148, p. 124 -5

[8] S. Davies, *The Four Branches of the Mabinogi* (Llandysul: Gomer Press, 1993), pp. 79-80.

Once she is acting with agency, upon Lleu's return, Blodeuwedd discovers what she must do to kill Lleu by leading him to believe that she is overcome with concern for him. The unsuspecting Lleu is touched by his wife's concern for him, and proceeds to tell her the specific details of how he can be killed.

> "'I cannot be killed indoors,' [Lleu] said, 'nor out of doors; I cannot be killed on horseback nor on foot.'
>
> 'Well,' [Blodeuwedd] said, "how can you be killed?'
>
> 'I will tell you,' he said. 'By making a bath for me on a riverbank, and constructing an arched roof above the tub, and then thatching that well and watertight. And by bringing a billy-goat,' he said, 'and standing it beside the tub; and I place one foot on the back of the billy-goat and the other on the edge of the tub. Whoever should strike me in that position would bring about my death'"[9]

In addition to these conditions, Lleu must also be struck with a spear created over the course of a year during Sunday mass in order to be killed. Blodeuwedd sends word to Gronw, who begins work on the spear, and when it is ready, Blodeuwedd sets up the required elements on the bank of the river Cynfael. She induces Lleu to get into position, when he is struck by the spear thrown by the waiting Gronw. The circumstances leading to Lleu's death are just as improbable as those which lead to his birth. Like many solar heroes, a magical weapon is required to defeat Lleu, and it is the creation and use of this weapon by Gronw that fulfils the last challenge of Sovereignty: the casting of the phallic spear symbolically imposes his virility over Lleu's, and almost mortally wounding Lleu instead turning him into an eagle with rotting flesh, indicating his unfitness to rule. Only once these challenges are met does Blodeuwedd go with Gronw to rule with him over the lands of Penllyn and Ardudwy, granting her new husband sovereignty over Lleu's former lands.

Blodeuwedd as Giver and Taker of Sovereignty

The Fourth Branch does not give a clear reason for Blodeuwedd's withdrawal of favour from Lleu, other than her becoming "filled with love" for Gronw.[10] In Irish lore, when Sovereignty withdraws her support from a king, it is either because he is an unrighteous ruler, or because of some kind of physical flaw —be it injury, illness, or deformity. The Fourth Branch states that after Lleu marries Blodeuwedd, "Math gave him the cantref of Dinoding to rule over.

---

[9] S. Davies, *The Mabinogion*, p. 60
[10] Ibid., p. 59

Lleu set up court in the cantref at a place called Mur Castell, in the uplands of Ardudwy; he settled there and ruled. And everyone was pleased with him and his governance."[11] Lleu was clearly not an unjust ruler, nor was he physically compromised, although after Blodeuwedd has run off with Gronw, Lleu is shown in the form of a wounded eagle, with rotting flesh falling off of his body;[12] either this is an indication of his unfitness to rule, or else a reflection of his broken relationship with Sovereignty at this time.

However, since Lleu was neither an unrighteous lord nor did he yet have any physical wounds, perhaps the alternative is that the reasons for the withdrawal of Sovereignty in the Fourth Branch does not follow the form typically seen in Irish legend. Rather, it seems to follow what Will Parker calls the "Near Eastern" model, where Sovereignty operates on a periodic shift of kingship based on the seasons, rather than an aperiodic shift, based upon the king's fitness to rule.[13]

There may be some significance in the fact that the very day that Lleu leaves his court to visit his uncle Math—and although the text is unclear, it could well be the first time Lleu has left his own court—is the day we meet Gronw hunting on Lleu's land. The lord of neighbouring Penllyn is chasing a stag, a mytheme which is associated with the encroachment of the Otherworld into this world, and which also heralds a coming encounter with Sovereignty. The withdrawal of Lleu from his holdings, whose name means "light" and whose character can be interpreted as a representation of the Solar Hero motif, may represent the departure of the light from the land—the summer leaving to make way for winter. Gronw, as Otherworldly hunter, not only arrives in Lleu's lands on the same day that Lleu departs, but we meet Gronw at a boundary place—the Cynfael river where he slays and dresses the stag. Further, it is dusk, a boundary time, when Gronw arrives at Lleu's court where Sovereignty, in the person of Blodeuwedd, offers him hospitality.

Blodeuwedd and Shape Changing

In typical tales, just as the king's fitness to rule is proved or disproved by the status of the land's prosperity, the physical appearance of Sovereignty is likewise a reflection of the relationship between the land and its king. When the land is without a righteous king, Sovereignty appears to potential successors in the aspect of a hag or loathly lady, and in this guise, whose hideous nature cannot

---

[11] S. Davies, *The Mabinogion*, p. 59
[12] Ibid., p. 62
[13] W. Parker, *The Four Branches of the Mabinogi* (California: Bardic Press, 2005), p. 386

be overstated in the various narratives, tests the would-be-kings, often by asking for a kiss or initiating sexual contact. However, when the land is wedded to its righteous and rightful king, Sovereignty transforms into a young and beautiful woman. It is not clear whether this transformation occurs because the representative of sovereignty receives some sort of transformative energy from the king, or if she changes aspect of her own volition, to symbolize her acceptance of the new king and the resulting revitalization of the land.

Shape-changing and illusion play significant roles in the Fourth Branch; we witness the manipulative glamours of Gwydion start wars and overcome destinies, Math's magical punitive transformations of Gwydion and Gilfaethwy into animals who bear each other sons, Aranrhod's son Dylan becoming a creature of the sea, and of course the mortally-wounded Lleu taking on the form of a sickly eagle. In almost all cases, the changes and transformations are temporary, except for the punishment that Gwydion visits upon Blodeuwedd for her role in betraying Lleu. In the text, we see him transforming her into an owl:

> "I will not kill you. I will do worse. Namely, I will release you in the form of a bird," he said. "And because of the shame you have brought upon Lleu Llaw Gyffes, you will never dare show your face in daylight for fear of all the birds. And all the birds will be hostile towards you. And it shall be their nature to strike you and molest you wherever they find you. You shall not lose your name, however, but shall always be called 'Blodeuwedd'." *Blodeuwedd* is owl in today's language. And for that reason birds hate the owl; and the owl is still called *Blodeuwedd*.[14]

There is a fundamental injustice in Gwydion's actions here, considering that his own transformational punishments were finite in duration, even though he instigated an unjust war which ended countless lives. Blodeuwedd, on the other hand, is punished indefinitely for "shaming Lleu Llaw Gyffes", and while it is true that she tried to have her husband killed, she did not actually succeed, making her punishment appear to be out of balance with her crime, especially when weighed against Gwydion's own transgressions. Perhaps the reason for this is that women are held to a different standard than men, and certainly Gwydion spends a great deal of the Fourth Branch circumventing or directly co-opting women's privileges and powers. Alternatively, there may be more being played out in this scene than is obvious on the surface.

In *Culhwch ac Olwen*, another medieval Welsh tale often collected in volumes along with the Four Branches, the Owl of Cwm Cawlwyd is established as

---

[14] S. Davies, *The Mabinogion*, p. 63

one of the Oldest Animals, along with the Blackbird of Cilgwari, the Stag of Rhedynfre, the Eagle of Gwernabwy, and the Salmon of Llyn Lliw.[15] Here the owl is depicted as a helpful and respected elder, quite different from the reviled bird described by Gwydion in the Fourth Branch. Indeed, in most cultures, the owl is a symbol of wisdom, and it often also holds associations with the night and magical arts. This nocturnal aspect is mentioned by Gwydion, and may prove to be the key to unlocking the subtextual key to understanding Blodeuwedd and her role in the seasonal procession, for the aspect she takes changes to reflect the man with whom she is partnered. She is the Flower Aspect, Blodeuedd when she is paired with Lleu, the Solar Hero who represents the Light, and, she is the Flower Faced owl, Blodeuwedd, when she is coupled with the Otherworldly Champion, Gronw the hunter, whose chthonic associations see him allied with the Dark, as we will see.

This concept of Seasonal Sovereignty, represented by the contest of suitors over the favour of a rule-granting maiden, is a motif which can be found in Irish, Welsh, and Arthurian legends. Kingly sacrifice and succession through combat are themes that are present in the Fourth Branch of the Mabinogi, and are key motifs to explore in order to understand the subtextual allegory of seasonal Sovereignty to be found in the tale. The motif of the *eniautos daimon* —a spirit or character who embodies the annual cycles of nature as they move through the stages of life: birth, challenge, death, and rebirth[16]—may also be underscoring aspects of the tale, as we shall see.

Sacred Kingship in the Fourth Branch

The rivalry between Lleu Llaw Gyffes and Gronw Pebyr in the Fourth Branch engenders a series of mirrored reversals between the two men; as one falls the other ascends, until their fortunes switch once more. In one of many examples of mirroring between Lleu and Gronw, they both symbolically establish, or at least presage, their sacred kingship through the killing of protected animals associated with royalty; in effect, the animals become the sacrificial proxy for their respective kings.

The Killing of the Wren

In the Fourth Branch, Gwydion and the yet-unnamed Lleu journey to Caer

---

[15] S. Davies, *The Mabinogion*, p. 204

[16] S. Arlen, *The Cambridge Ritualists: an annotated bibliography of the works by and about Jane Ellen Harrison, Gilbert Murray, Francis M. Cornford, and Arthur Bernard Cook* (Metuchen, New Jersey: Scarecrow Press, 1990), p. 2

Aranrhod disguised as shoemakers in a ship conjured from seaweed using Gwydion's magic. After two purposefully botched attempts at making a pair of fine shoes for Aranrhod, the boy's mother, using only her measurements, she at last boards the ship to ensure the shoemakers can make them to her correct size. Almost immediately after her arrival, a wren lands on the ship and the boy strikes it with a stone. Impressed at his skill, Aranrhod laughs:

> "God knows," she said, "it is with a skilful hand the fair-haired one has hit it!"
> "Indeed," [Gwydion] said, "And God's curse be upon you. He has now got a name, and it's good enough. From now on, he is Lleu Llaw Gyffes."[17]

This episode is important both because it sees Gwydion overcome one of the *tengyd* or destinies which Aranrhod has placed on her son—that he will have no name until he gets one from her—and because of the significance of the bird which is felled by Lleu; indeed, the narrative is so deliberately specific in naming the wren particularly, that it must hold a meaning greater than showing off the skill of the boy in hitting a small bird with a stone. To understand, we must examine the legends and lore surrounding the wren, much of which would likely have been known to the medieval Welsh audience of the Fourth Branch, who would have therefore understood the deeper significance of this action.

The wren, a tiny bird known for its reproductive prowess and which famously makes its nests in or close to the ground, was a symbol of fertility.[18] An honoured and protected species in medieval times, it was considered bad luck to harm a wren or disturb its nest, and this notion is attested to in folk sayings such as:

> *Y neb a dorro nyth y dryw*
> *Ni chaiff iechayd yn ei fyw*
>
> Whoever robs the wren's nest shall
> Never have wealth in his life[19]

Reviewing the names given to the wren in many parts of Europe, it is clear

---

[17] S. Davies, *The Mabinogion*, p. 56
[18] E. Lawrence, *Hunting the Wren: Transformation of Bird to Symbol* (Knoxville: University of Tennessee Press, 1997), p. 32
[19] I. Peate, "The Wren in Welsh Folklore," Man, Vol. 36 (Jan 1936), p. 3

that the bird was held in high regard, and its connection with royalty appears to be almost universal. In many languages the name for the wren glosses back to mean "king"; we see it in Greek (basiliskos, "little king"), Latin (regulus, "king"), French (roitelet, "little king"), Spanish (reyezuelo, "little king"), Italian (reatino, "little king"), Danish (elle-konge, "alder king"), Dutch (konije, "king" or winter-koninkje, "winter king"), German (zaunkonig, "hedge king"), Teutonic (konig vogel, "king of birds") and so on.[20]

A Manx folk-tale recounts how it is the wren became king. All of the birds had gathered together to decide, once and for all, who would be first among them. In turn, each bird came forward to state what gifts they had which set them above all of the rest. Although the wren had proven her cleverness to the approval of the gathering, the eagle suggested that the bird who could fly the highest should be the one to rule over them all. The gathered birds agreed, and the eagle flew up as high as he could, far surpassing all of the rest. He called out to the assembly, "I am King of the Birds, King of the Birds!"—but he didn't realize that the wren had hidden herself among his feathers, and as he made his proclamation, she jumped up to the top of his head and cried out, "Not so, not so, I'm above him, I'm above him!" And thus, through her cleverness, the wren became king of the birds.[21]

Given its protected status and stature as king of the birds, the tradition of the Wren Hunt found in the British Isles, Ireland, and France seems almost counter intuitive, and indeed it is an example of a ritual which countermands the usual order of things. There are many variations of the Wren Hunt, but there are several elements which most traditions have in common: it is a winter tradition, which typically took place sometime between the Winter Solstice and Twelfth Night, although in some places it could happen as far out as Imbolc and St. Valentine's Day; it was made up of two phases—the hunting of the bird by local youths, and then the subsequent display and parading of the animal in a kind of wassailing celebration; the first person to capture or kill the wren held a position of honour, acting, for example, as king of the celebrations the following day; this "king" was sometimes considered to be blessed with good luck in the year to come, and had the ability to bestow fortune and fertility on others.[22] These abilities are very similar to those of a king who has undertaken the *hieros gamos*, or sacred marriage, with a representative of Sovereignty.

---

[20] E. Lawrence, p. 32
[21] S. Morrison, *Manx Fairy Tales* (London: David Nutt, 1911. Available at http://www.isle-of-man.com/manxnotebook/fulltext/sm1911/p123.htm <Accessed 10 September, 2014>, p. 123
[22] E. Lawrence, p. 123

The wren's connection with royalty is important when considering some of the theories surrounding the purpose of the Wren Hunt. In *The Golden Bough*, Frazer talks about the hunting of the wren along with several examples of similar ritual behaviour from other cultures around the world. Believing that the wren stood as proxy for an ancient tradition where the annual king would be sacrificed at year's end to ensure the abundance of the crops and animals in the year to come, Frazer writes:

> The worshipful animal is killed with special solemnity once a year; and before or immediately after death he is promenaded from door to door, that each of his worshippers may receive a portion of the divine virtues that are supposed to emanate from the dead or dying god. Religious processings of this sort must have had a great place in the ritual of European peoples in prehistoric times, if we may judge from the numerous traces of them which have survived in folk custom.[23]

Armstrong argues the significance of the Wren Hunt occurring near or around the Winter Solstice, saying that it is a "New Year ceremonial having as its purpose the defeat of the dark-earth powers and identification with the hoped-for triumph of light and life."[24] This connection with fertility and light may also have its roots in the Roman celebration of Saturnalia, and indeed, cultures around the world have celebrated the rebirth of the light at this, the period of the year with the longest nights. The tradition of the Wren Hunt may have its roots in reaction to the liminality of the winter season, a time period which may have been perceived as dangerous in ancient times. It may have been believed that the temporal transition represented by the new year required human assistance, in this case through ritual sacrifice, both to achieve the shift from the old order to the new, as well as to do so with as much good fortune and abundance as possible.[25]

Whether or not the wren is a stand in for a human sacrifice, it is believed to have represented the energies of the old year, and through its killing, the new year was able to begin. It is significant that a common feature of the Welsh "Wren House"—the small glass-sided house mounted on a pole and used to carry the wren in procession—is a ribbon-bedecked four-spoked wheel, a symbol, Eliade asserts, represents the year and its four seasons.[26] Further, he

---

[23] J. Frazer, *The Golden Bough* (New York: Collier Books, Macmillan Publishing Company, 1963), p. 623

[24] E. Armstrong, *The Folklore of Birds* (London: Dover Publications, second edn 1970), p. 161

[25] E. Lawrence, p. 30

[26] M. Eliade, *A History of Religious Ideas, Vol. 2: From Gautama Buddha to the Triumph of Christianity,* trans. Willard R. Trask (Chicago: University of Chicago Press,1982), p. 142

states that "the terms designating the 'wheel' and the 'year' are identical in Celtic languages."[27]

A traditional Wren Carol from Pembrokeshire clearly conflates the wren and kingship with the passing of the old year into the new:

> Joy, health, love and peace be all here in this place.
> By your leave we will sing concerning our King.
>
> Our King is well dressed, in silks of the best,
> In ribbons so rare, no king can compare.
>
> We have travelled many miles, over hedges and stiles,
> In search of our King, unto you we bring.
>
> Old Christmas is past, Twelfth Night is the last,
> And we bid you adieu, great joy to the new.[28]

Perhaps, then, the redactor of the Fourth Branch was deliberately linking Lleu's action to the proxy killing of the wren, thereby marking him as the representative of the new order; by killing the wren, associated with earthy chthonic forces and the darkness of winter, Lleu becomes the new king. Fife writes:

> The wren is the spirit of the Old Year, killed at the Winter Solstice. The new year rises up like an eagle, just as Lleu Llaw Gyffes' soul becomes an eagle, and the wren rides up on the eagle's back just as one year runs into the next.[29]

Lleu's kingship will be validated later on in the Fourth Branch, when he marries the Flower Bride who is the embodiment of the Sovereignty of the land. The symbolic act of killing the wren, however, not only marks him as the new king, but ties him into the seasonal progression, for if the death of the king of the birds heralds the end of winter, so then is the new king the representation of summer. In Lleu's case, this is quite appropriate for it is the act of killing the wren which earns him his name, which can be translated to mean "light." This is especially fitting when we recall that in ancient times, it is believed that people in Celtic lands originally had only two seasons, winter and summer, which were considered the dark and light halves of the year.[30]

---

[27] M. Eliade, p. 144

[28] E. Lawrence, p. 112

[29] G. Fife, *Arthur the King* (New York: Sterling Publishing, 1991), p. 155

[30] A. Rees, and B. Rees, *Celtic Heritage: Ancient Tradition in Ireland and Wales* (London: Thames and Hudson, Ltd., 1961), p. 84

The Wild Hunt

In the last third of the Fourth Branch we meet Gronw Pebyr, the lord of Penllyn which borders the now-married Lleu's lands of Ardudwy. He is engaged in the hunt of a stag on Lleu's land, and when Gronw and his dogs finally fell the beast, they do so on the banks of the Cynfael river. This introduction to Gronw, albeit brief, is dense with symbolism, and we can understand a great deal about his allegorical nature through examining parallel folkloric motifs found in other Welsh tales.

Let us first consider the symbolism of the stag. Because of the periodic shedding of its antlers, the stag is connected to the turning of the seasons.[31] As one of the Oldest Animals enumerated in *Culhwch and Olwen,*[32] the stag appears to have been considered a mythical ancestor for the Celtic Britons, and holds strong associations with fertility. It was further, according to Eliade, a "funerary animal and guide for the dead",[33] and so the stag appears to have represented the essence of both death and rebirth. "Finally," Eliade writes, "it was the game animal preferred above all others by kings and heroes, and the death at the end of the hunt was symbolically one with the tragic death of heroes",[34] and so again, we see a sacred animal being conflated with a royal, seasonal sacrifice.

Like Lleu's killing of the wren, the stag hunt is layered with meaning, and like the wren, the stag appears to have been venerated as a royal proxy for the sacrifice of the king. "The veneration shown for the wren as a royal bird is paralleled by the chivalrous respect for the stag as royal game and also by strict game laws ... which made the hunting of the stag a royal prerogative."[35] As with most sacrificial animals, the stag held a liminal quality, representing both death and life, and also heralded the blurring of the boundaries between this world and the Otherworld, known in Welsh mythos as Annwfn. Gruffydd admits it is difficult to define what Annwfn meant precisely to the Celtic Britons, but notes that this Otherworld of gods and heroes is sometimes "regarded as the Land of the Dead, something like the Greek Hades, presided over by 'dark' divinities; sometimes it is the land of Youth and Promise, Tir na nOg, the home of bliss and harmony; sometimes it is a mysterious border country, menacing

---

[31] M. Green, *The Gods of the Celts* (Phoenix Mill, Sutton Publishing Ltd., 2004), p. 172
[32] S. Davies, *The Mabinogion*, p. 203-4
[33] M. Eliade, p. 147
[34] Ibid., p. 147
[35] E. Lawrence, p. 138

the land of the living, the actual world."[36] It is this latter that is the most closely represented aspect of Annwfn presented in the Four Branches.

In the First Branch of *Y Mabinogi*, a stag hunt brings together Pwyll, Prince of Dyfed, and Arawn, King of Annwfn. The influence of the Otherworld is underscored by the coloration of Arawn's dogs; they are white with red ears, a colour combination often used in Celtic tradition to indicate the presence of the supernatural.[37] Pwyll insults Arawn by calling off the Annuvian king's dogs in order to feed his own with the felled stag. To make amends for his deed, Pwyll agrees to switch places with Arawn; he will take on Arawn's likeness and rule Annwfn in his stead for a year and a day. At the end of this time, Pwyll is to battle Arawn's enemy, Hafgan, a neighbouring king from Annwfn with whom Arawn is locked in eternal combat.[38] When the two rivals meet at the appointed place—a ford that borders their two kingdoms—the disguised Pwyll follows the instruction given to him by Arawn, and deals but one blow to Hafgan, no matter how much the stricken king begs otherwise, for only thus could he be defeated. By vanquishing Hafgan, Pwyll unites all of Annwfn and turns the kingdom back over to Arawn. When he returns to Dyfed once more, Pwyll learns that it had been ruled well in his stead, and through his own just rule of Annwfn and the defeat of Hafgan, Pwyll has earned the friendship of Arawn, as well as the title of Pen Annwfn—the Head of Annwfn.[39]

Similarly, in the Fourth Branch, not only do we see a stag hunt and an encounter with a neighbouring lord, but Gronw's killing of the stag takes place on the banks of a river, just as the battle between Pwyll and Hafgan occurs at a ford. This is significant not only because of the liminal qualities presented by these border areas, but also because of the association with water; bodies of water and places of transition were both believed to be areas where one could enter into the Otherworld. While the events of the Fourth Branch do not, unlike the First Branch, explicitly state that they are taking place in the Otherworld, it is possible that the contemporary audience may have made that connection based on what appears to be several common motifs in medieval literature.

In his annotations for *The Four Branches of the Mabinogi*, Parker refers to the the work of Bromwich, who identified the mytheme called "The Chase of the White Stag" which, to the medieval Welsh audience, served as a readily recognizable marker heralding the entrance into or involvement with the

[36] W.J. Gruffydd, *Folklore and Myth in the Mabinogion* (Cardiff: University of Wales Press, 1958), p. 8

[37] S. Davies, *The Mabinogion*, p. 228

[38] Ibid., p. 4

[39] Ibid., p. 8

Otherworld. Further, this particular motif often leads to an encounter between the hero and a woman who is a representative of the Sovereignty of the land, or else it was the prelude to a situation where the figures from the Otherworld sought out the assistance of the hero to help resolve issues back in their own kingdoms, as in the First Branch exchange between Pwyll and Arawn.[40] It is the hunt as a symbolic signpost for a forthcoming connection with sovereignty which holds the most application in the Fourth Branch, as we will see.

Several of the narrative features found in the First and Fourth Branches are also present in tales relating to Gwyn ap Nudd. Primarily known to us in an early Arthurian context from *Culhwch ac Olwen*, Gwyn also features in Welsh folklore as the leader of the Wild Hunt, and is depicted as the Fairy King of Annwfn in *The Life of Saint Collen*.[41] The Wild Hunt is an international folk motif (classification E501) that is found across the British Isles and Europe. It has many different variations, but the core motif is that of a ghostly hunter, often accompanied by baying hounds, which rides across the land in pursuit of prey. The object of the pursuit differs from place to place, and the reason for the hunt varies; sometimes the hunter is a nobleman or king, other times he is a tragic figure trying to make amends for wrongdoing in life, or else to avenge a wrong done to him. The Wild Hunt features especially strongly in the myths and legends of Wales and England from the twelfth century onward.[42] As leader of the Wild Hunt, and Lord of the Underworld, Gwyn is said to ride out from the Otherworld with the *Cwn Annwn*, the Hounds of Annwn, every Calan Gaeaf in order to gather the souls of all who had died in the newly-ending year, and bring them back to the Otherworld with him.[43] MacCana calls Gwyn "a 'magic warrior-huntsman' and leader of the otherworld folk."[44]

In *Culhwch ac Olwen*, Gwyn is a warrior in Arthur's retinue, though his story contains hints of his chthonic attributes. When gathering the warriors and resources necessary to hunt Twrch Trwyth, a magical boar from whom Arthur's men needed to obtain a comb and shears in order to satisfy a quest, Gwyn is named as being necessary for the campaign, and is described thus: "Twrch Trwyth will not be hunted until Gwyn son of Nudd is found—God has

[40] W. Parker, p. 233

[41] B. Roberts,"*Culhwch ac Olwen*, the Triads, Saints' Lives" in R. Bromwich, A.O.H. Jarman, and B.F. Roberts, eds., *The Arthur of the Welsh: The Arthurian Legend in Medieval Welsh Literature* (Cardiff: University of Wales Press, 1991), p. 190

[42] C. Lindahl; J. McNamara; and J. Lindow, eds. *Medieval Folklore* (Oxford: Oxford University Press, 2002), p. 432

[43] R. Gwyndaf, *Welsh Folk Tales* (Cardiff: National Museums and Galleries of Wales, 1999), p. 73

[44] P. MacCana, *Celtic Mythology* (London: Hamilin Publishing Group, 1970), p. 100

put the spirit of the demons of Annwfn in him, lest the world be destroyed. He will not be spared from there."[45] He is described as a fierce warrior in *Culhwch ac Olwen*; his skills as a huntsman and rider are especially emphasized. Gwyn is depicted engaging in rather extreme forms of vengeance in the text: "And he captured Pen son of Nethog, and Nwython, and Cyledyr Wyllt his son, and he killed Nwython and cut out his heart, and forced Cyledyr to eat his father's heart, and because of this Cyledyr went mad."[46]

This combination of motifs—a contest between rival suitors or neighbouring kings, taking place at liminal times and/or in boundary places, and chthonic otherworldly influences symbolized by an iteration of the Wild Hunt— suggests that like Gwyn and Arawn before him, Gronw is an Otherworldly figure, and as such, can be identified with the dark half of the year.

Solar Hero and Otherworldly Champion

Lleu and Gronw appear to conform to a pattern of rivals that we see over and over again in tales from Celtic lands, representing a moiety complex of correspondences which are interrelated symbolically. On the one hand, we have the archetype of the Solar Hero, who is often, but not always, the protagonist of the story. He holds associations with the natural world, with the forces of order, with daytime, with the summer, with fertility and life, and with various solar symbols including oak trees and eagles. On the other hand, we have the archetype of the Otherworldly Champion, who is often, but not always, the antagonist of the story—or who, at least, stands in challenge to the Solar Hero. The Otherworldly Champion holds association with the supernatural, with the forces of disorder or reversal, with night-time, with the winter, with the harvest and with death, and with various Otherworldly symbols including stags and evergreen plants such as holly, ivy, and conifers in general. Here is a chart of correspondences often associated with these two archetypes:

Solar Hero	Otherworldly Champion
Protagonist	Antagonist or Challenger
Natural World	Supernatural World
Warrior	Magician
Order	Disorder or Reversal
Fertility	Harvest
Life	Death
Summer	Winter

---

[45] S. Davies, *The Mabinogion*, p. 199
[46] Ibid., p. 207

Light	Dark
Oak	Evergreens
Eagle	Stag

Meetings between these rivals often take place at boundary times—such as at nightfall or on spirit nights like May Day or November Eve—or at threshold places—such as at fords or on river banks. Typically their disputes have to do with claiming dominion, either indirectly as in the form of a love interest or a land dispute, or directly with a literal representative of the Sovereignty Goddess or spirit of the land. Reversals of fortune seem to characterize their meetings, often in such a way as their fates coming to mirror each other. There is often a seasonal quality about their rivalry, with their battles occurring at the same time in the same place every year, or else they face off against each other on a threshold day which marks the transition between the summer and winter.

The Hero and the Champion in the Fourth Branch

To continue with this paradigm of dualities in the Fourth Branch, Lleu establishes himself as the Solar Hero, representing the light half of the year by killing the wren. Similarly, Gronw demonstrates he is an iteration of the Otherworldly Champion by engaging in a stag hunt across borders in an echo of Arawn from the First Branch. The first reversal of Lleu's fortune sees him move from his lack of social status to a being fully integrated into society. Overcoming the *tyngedau* placed upon him by his mother, Lleu comes into his own with the help of Gwydion; he fulfils his potential for kingship and gains a cantref to rule over after he obtains a name, his arms, and a wife. As portended when he overcame the wren, that symbol of winter, summer triumphs.

The second reversal concerning Lleu occurs when he is felled by the magical spear forged by Gronw during a year's worth of Sunday masses, a time when such work is forbidden. The circumstances that would lead to Lleu's death require that he be in a liminal place—neither indoors, nor out; neither on foot nor on horseback—conditions all met by the milieu set up by Blodeuwedd on the banks of the Cynfael river, another threshold place. Yet another iteration of reversal can be found here, for this is the place where, earlier in the tale, Gronw killed and dressed the stag he hunted before calling at Lleu's court; symbolically, then, Gronw has wrested away the sovereignty from Lleu in the same place Gronw demonstrated his own Otherworldly kingship. Indeed, once Lleu flies away in the form of a wounded eagle—a solar totem which, in this case, some have associated with Lleu's soul—Gronw departs with Blodeuwedd, they sleep together at his court, and Gronw takes lordship over Lleu's lands. Winter has triumphed over summer.

Word of these happenings reach Gwydion and he searches for Lleu, finally following a sow to an oak tree that shelters an eagle with rotting flesh high up in its branches. The oak tree, like the eagle, is associated with sky gods and solar divinities in many European cultures—Roman Jupiter, for example —giving us a reiteration of Lleu's status.[47] Gwydion chants three *englynion* to coax the wounded eagle down from the top of the tree, which appears to also dwell in a liminal place; the oak tree is between two lakes, and it cannot be wetted by the rain, nor can it be melted by heat. When the eagle hops into his lap, Gwydion uses his wand to change the bird back into Lleu's human form; so wounded is he, it takes all of the best physicians in Gwynedd to heal him "before the end of the year."[48] After being restored to health, Lleu seeks recompense from Gronw for all that has transpired; Lleu's demands set up the third reversal, and although Gronw offers him treasure and land to make peace between them, Lleu refuses, saying that Gronw "must come to where I was when he threw the spear at me, while I stand where he was. And he must let me throw a spear at him."[49]

In the end, the two men face each other, once more on the banks of the Cynfael river. Gronw makes one last appeal to Lleu, asking that he be able to hold a stone from the riverbank between himself and Lleu, because everything that had happened between them had transpired because of a woman. Lleu grants Gronw his request, and casts the spear at Gronw, which pierces the stone and Gronw both, breaking his back and killing him. "Then Lleu Llaw Gyffes took possession of his land for a second time, and ruled over it prosperously. And according to the tale, he was lord over Gwynedd after that."[50] With this final reversal, which occurs at the same threshold place where Gronw kills the stag, and where a year later he critically wounds Lleu, the Solar Hero has obtained sovereignty over his lands once more, and the Otherworldly Champion has been sent back into the chthonic darkness. Summer has triumphed over winter once more.

Lleu goes on to rule justly, although no mention is made of his taking a wife; at this point in the tale Blodeuwedd has already been turned into an owl, ostensibly forever. There are several possible explanations for Lleu's lack of a mate, if we rule out authorial negligence or subsequent explanation found in a now-missing tale. One option is that Aranrhod's *tengyd* still holds, and Blodeuwedd's transformation has left Lleu without a suitable candidate for

---

[47] M. Green, *The Gods of the Celts*, p. 50
[48] S. Davies, *The Mabinogion*, p. 62-63
[49] Ibid., p. 64
[50] Ibid., p. 64

marriage, and Gwydion has chosen not to create a new one for him. Another option is that Lleu has followed in the footsteps of Gwydion and Math in their penchant for co-opting female power; as such, he may no longer need Sovereignty's partnership to rule. If this latter is the case, there still appears to be evidence of the old order as Lleu's eventual rule over Gwynedd seems to be a result of matrilineal inheritance.

Although it is not directly mentioned in the text, we see Gwydion, Math's sister's son, acting as Math's heir at the beginning of the Fourth Branch, so we may conclude that Gwydion does become lord of Gwynedd after Math's death. If this is the case, then it would follow that Lleu, Gwydion's sister's son, takes the throne of Gwynedd as Gwydion's heir. Alternatively, if Lleu is biologically Gwydion's son, as some believe the subtext of the Fourth Branch suggests, perhaps Gwydion *has* succeeded in what Sheehan has suggested is the underlying struggle of the Fourth Branch—the new patrilineal order seeking to overwrite matriliny— and that Lleu inherits directly from Gwydion, not because Gwydion is his uncle, but because Gwydion is his father.[51] Another option is that the tale is left open ended because the cycle simply repeats itself; when Lleu is lord, Blodeuwedd returns to her flower aspect, when the reversal happens once more, Blodeuwedd's partnership of Gronw sees her return to her owl form.

Seasonal Triangle

Unlike the majority of representations of Sovereignty in Celtic mythos, who gives and takes the right to rule based on the fitness of the king, Blodeuwedd appears to conform to what Parker has called the "Near Eastern" type, which grants and repeals the kingship on a seasonal basis.[52] Like other Sovereignty figures, she changes her shape as a reflection of her relationship with the king, but in her case, rather than being beautiful when she is with the rightful king and loathly when the land is without a righteous ruler, Blodeuwedd's form, and even her name, is a reflection of which of the two rivals with whom she is partnered.

When she is married to Lleu, the Solar Hero whose very name means "light", she is Blodeuedd, "flower aspect"—a fitting name, for does not the flower seek out the light of the sun? When she is married to Gronw, the Otherworldly Champion, she takes on the aspect of the owl and is renamed "Blodeuwedd" —after a type of owl which to this day bears her name in Wales.

---

[51] S. Sheehan, "Matrilineal Subjects", p. 337
[52] W. Parker, p. 387

This latter is especially provocative when we recall the ways in which Gronw shares attributes with Otherworldly lords, including Arawn and Gwyn ap Nudd. All three of them are associated with the hunt—both Gronw and Arawn with the stag hunt, and Gwynn with the Wild Hunt—but Gwyn may have an additional association, that of the owl. In his poem "The Owl", early 14th century Welsh poet Dafydd ap Gwilym links the owl with Gwyn, while also alluding to Blodeuwedd in her owl form:

> "Woe for her song (a wooden-collared roebuck),
> And her face (features of a gentle woman),
> And her shape; she's the phantom of the birds.
> Every bird attacks her — she's dirty and she's exiled:
> Is it not strange that she is alive?
>
> This one chatters on a hillside more
> At night than does, in a wood, a nightingale.
> By day she will not draw (a firm belief)
> Her head from a sturdy hollow tree.
>
> Eloquently she used to howl—I know her face
> She is a bird of Gwyn ap Nudd.
> Garrulous owl that sings to thieves—
> Bad luck to her tongue and tone!"[53]

The lines "every bird attacks her" and "by day she will not draw (a firm belief) her head from a sturdy hollow tree" seems to refer to the curse Gwydion lays upon Blodeuwedd as she is transformed, saying "And because of the shame you have brought upon Lleu Llaw Gyffes, you will never dare show your face in daylight for fear of all the birds. And all the birds will be hostile to you. And it shall be in their nature to strike you and molest you wherever they find you."[54] Dafydd was likely aware of this passage in the Fourth Branch, but it is unknown if the connection with the owl in general or Blodeuwedd in particular is a traditional association with Gwyn or was the result of poetic inspiration on the part of Dafydd. Either way, the nocturnal hunting bird seems a logical companion for an Otherworldly Champion like Gwyn—and like Gronw.

Reclaiming Blodeuwedd

With her role taken in this light, we can envisage Blodeuwedd as the Lady

---

[53] G. Thomas, trans. *Dafydd ap Gwilym: His Poems,* (Cardiff: University of Wales Press, 2001), p. 57-58
[54] S. Davies, *The Mabinogion*, p. 62

of Seasonal Sovereignty and the axis around which the wheel of the seasons turns; she is in her flower aspect during the Light Half of the year, and in her owl aspect during the Dark Half. As with Blodeuwedd, although we must seek out other examples of Seasonal Sovereignty in the subtext of other tales—and there are others which we have not explored here—we can see that there is a pattern which reveals itself, and which may qualify the concept of Seasonal Sovereignty as a motif of its own. Further, it may serve to inspire a re-visioning of the reputations of these types of Sovereignty figures, rehabilitating these female characters by freeing them from the overly simplistic motif of the Unfaithful Wife and seeing the empowering role they truly play.

BIBLIOGRAPHY

Primary Sources

Culhwch and Olwen: An Edition and Study of the Oldest Arthurian Tale, Rachel Bromwich and D. Simon Evans, eds. (Cardiff: University of Wales Press, 1992).

Dafydd ap Gwilym: His Poems, translated by Gwyn Thomas, (Cardiff: University of Wales Press, 2001).

The Laws of Hywel Dda (Continued), *The Cambro-Briton,* Vol. 2, No. 21 (May, 1821), pp. 393-399.

The Mabinogion, translated by Sioned Davies, (New York: Oxford University Press, 2007).

The Physicians of Myddfai, translated by John Pughe, (Felinfach:Llanerch Publishers, 1993). Facimile reprint.

Preiddeu Annwn: The Spoils of Annwn, Sarah Higley, trans. (Rochester: University of Rochester The Camelot Project, 2007. Available at http://d.lib. rochester.edu/camelot/text/preiddeu-annwn.

"The Tragic Death of Cu Roi mac Dairi", *Ancient Irish Tales.* ed. and trans. by Tom P. Cross & Clark Harris Slover (New York: Henry Holt & Co., 1936). Available at http://www.maryjones.us/ctexts/curoi.html.

"The Wedding of Sir Gawain and Dame Ragnelle", *Sir Gawain: Eleven Romances and Tales*, Thomas Hahn, ed. (Kalamazoo, Michigan: Medieval Institute Publications, 1995). Available at http://d.lib.rochester.edu/teams/text/hahn-sir-gawain-wedding-of-sir-gawain-and-dame-ragnelle.

Secondary Sources

Adler, Alfred, "Sovereignty in Chrétien's Yvain", *PMLA*, Vol. 62, No. 2 (Jun., 1947), pp. 281-305.

Arlen, Shelley, *The Cambridge Ritualists: an annotated bibliography of the works by and about Jane Ellen Harrison, Gilbert Murray, Francis M. Cornford, and Arthur Bernard Cook* (Metuchen, New Jersey: Scarecrow Press, 1990).

Armstrong, Edward A., *The Folklore of Birds* (London: Dover Publications, second edn 1970).

Cartwright, Jane, *Feminine Sanctity and Spirituality in Medieval Wales* (Cardiff: University of Wales Press, 2008).

Davies, Sioned, *The Four Branches of the Mabinogi* (Llandysul: Gomer Press, 1993).

Eliade, Mircea, *A History of Religious Ideas, Vol. 2: From Gautama Buddha to the Triumph of Christianity*, trans. Willard R. Trask (Chicago: University of Chicago Press, 1982).

Ellis, T.P., "Legal references, terms and conceptions in the Mabinogion", *Y Cymmrodor* 39 (1928), 86 – 148.

Fife, Graeme, *Arthur the King* (New York: Sterling Publishing, 1991).

Frazer, James G., *The Golden Bough* (New York: Collier Books, Macmillan Publishing Company, 1963).

Green, Miranda, *The Gods of the Celts* (Phoenix Mill, Sutton Publishing Ltd., 2004).

Gruffydd, W.J., *Folklore and Myth in the Mabinogion* (Cardiff: University of Wales Press, 1958).

Gwyndaf, Robin, *Welsh Folk Tales* (Cardiff: National Museums and Galleries of Wales, 1999).

Lawrence, Elizabeth A., *Hunting the Wren: Transformation of Bird to Symbol* (Knoxville: University of Tennessee Press, 1997).

Lawton, Jocelyne, *Flowers and Fables: A Welsh Herbal* (Bridgend: Seren Books, 2006).

Lindahl, Carl; McNamara, John; and Lindow, John, eds. *Medieval Folklore* (Oxford:Oxford University Press, 2002).

Mac Cana, Proinsias, *Celtic Mythology* (London: Hamilin Publishing Group, 1970).

Morrison, Sophia, *Manx Fairy Tales* (London: David Nutt, 1911). Available at http://www.isle-of-man.com/manxnotebook/fulltext/sm1911/p123.htm <Accessed 10 September, 2014>.

Parker, Will, *The Four Branches of the Mabinogi* (California: Bardic Press, 2005).

Peate, Iorwerth C., "The Wren in Welsh Folklore", *Man*, Vol. 36 (Jan 1936), pp. 1 – 3.

Rees, Alwyn and Rees Brinley, *Celtic Heritage: Ancient Tradition in Ireland and Wales* (London: Thames and Hudson, Ltd., 1961).

Roberts, Brynley "*Culhwch ac Olwen*, the Triads, Saints' Lives" in R. Bromwich, A.O.H. Jarman, and B.F. Roberts,eds., *The Arthur of the Welsh: The Arthurian Legend in Medieval Welsh Literature* (Cardiff: University of Wales Press, 1991).

Sheehan, Sarah, "Matrilineal Subjects: Ambiguity, Bodies, and Metamorphosis in the Fourth Branch of the "Mabinogi"", *Signs*, 34 (2):(2009), pp. 319-342.

Transformation

BY LORI FELDMANN

I have lost, wept, lain in the dark,
I have dreamt about who I can be.
Then She who is owl and bride
Who has walked and now glides
Called out ever so softly to me:

Unfurl
Transform
Let your fear fall away
and leap
into the great unknown

Remember
Who you were
I promise you have wings
You merely forgot
You have already flown

And so I jumped,
And I fell,
And then I flew.

And still, I am flying...

She flies within me, above me, below me,
Lifting me up, watching me soar.
I am feathers and sight.
I am transformed in the light.
I am all that I dreamed of and more.

PHOTO CREDIT: JHENAH TELYNDRU

Tomen y Mur (The Mound in the Walls) - Although today the landscape is dominated by a Norman motte, this was once Mur-y-Castell (The Castle in the Walls), the court of Blodeuwedd and Lleu in Ardudwy mentioned in the Fourth Branch.

Lady Blodeuwedd, Be With Us Tonight

Maddi Jabin

Words and Music by Maddi Jabin © 2010. All rights reserved.

Night-Blooming

BY JENNIFER LAWRENCE

Flowers never really suited you, did they?

You didn't ask to be made, woven together
from beautiful but unsubstantial stuff:
Quickly blossoming, quickly fading,
Fair of face but weak of substance,
And made by men's magic not to exist in your own right,
But to be a thing -- a pretty decoration, a yielding toy,
Or at best a willing bedwarmer for yet another man.
"Wife", they might have called you,
but the name "slave" would have suited as well.

Which is to say, not at all.

It was assumed you'd be willing:
> grateful for your existence,
> grateful for any scrap of affection tossed in your direction,
> grateful to the ones who made you
>> as hounds must accept the scraps tossed from master's table.

But some hounds bite the hand that feeds them,
discontented with scraps,
deeming themselves more worthy of
not just the truth of love, nor of a fairer fare,
But unwilling to accept a life in a box made ready for them:
Do this, go there, fetch that,
And always, heel!

Was it simply that you worried where Lleu's eyes might turn
once your blossoms started to wilt?
I think not:
I think that those magicians, like all men,
Conflated 'wilt' with 'will',
Tried to bar the slow development of one
by barring the other,
and failed.

Slow, it grew within you, this thing called desire:
      this maddened mood--
      not merely desire for another form or face in your bed,
but the desire to have your own will.
Never had they asked you what your choice might have been,
to exist as field of blossoms, or maid of radiant beauty,
      or not at all.
And if they failed to take into account this elemental question,
then surely no other desire of yours did they concern themselves with.

So, yes, desire:
The desire to be more than just some pretty man's pretty toy,
the desire to make your own choices, born of free will,
the desire to set yourself apart from him, whatever the consequences,
And so you did.

A woman's sweet voice might wheedle all sorts of interesting information
      from one who should know better than to divulge such secrets;
Too, a woman's sweet voice -- sweeter than the nightingale,
      sweeter than the fragrance of meadowsweet -- might entice another man
      to put good use to such secrets:
            in the moment between night and day,
            neither inside nor outside,
            neither naked as a babe from the womb
            nor clothed in king's raiment,
            not on foot and not astride,
            and with no weapon made by the hand of lawful man.

In the end, did it matter much that the one who you were made for
      returned from the death that did not take him?
      Did it matter much, that the one you traded him for died instead?
      Did it matter much, that one of the magicians who made you
            tracked you down and changed those flowers to feathers?

After all, flowers never really suited you, did they?

Far better, the silent sweep of wing
        the strength of night-bird's claws,
        the eyes that pierce the darkness,
        the beak that pierces bone,
And better by far, the hunter's will that knows no master.

The white disc of your wide-eyed face blooms by night,
Fairer by far than the flowers of oak and broom and meadowsweet,
      -- and freer, as well.

She, Within Me

BY ADARA BRYN

You, Goddess-woman over there
You, with the flowers in your hair, your skin, your breath
You, with the wild heart, beating, yearning
You, with the soul-shining, ready-to-burst-out-of-your-skin raw beauty
You, with petals falling, feathers springing forth
Your spirit ready to soar
Emerging, becoming, thriving
All that was, all that is, all that will be
You, who cannot be contained
Goddess-woman there
Here
Within
Me

BLODEUWEDD

Fair Maiden, Bright Spring Queen

Sharone Marraccini

Words and Music by Sharone Marraccini ©2015. All rights reserved.

Meadowsweet / Passionflower

Sexual Passion as Blodeuwedd's Gift

BY TIFFANY LAZIC

"She alights on the rampart,
As meadowsweet on a light breeze.
The awakening sun kissing her cheek,
Warming the peace that hangs like a stone.

He breaks from the trees,
As fury on a stamping steed.
The glorious chase goading his heels,
Cracking stone with passion's hammer.

All the gentle words,
the demure looks,
the placid sighs,
the languid bows
Arch in mid-flight
As fire cracks Oak.

They are lost.
And found
In the heat of the other's eyes."

*T*here are so many levels to the myth of Blodeuwedd. The magic and mystery of Her creation. Her journey from Spirit into the form of a woman. The silence of Her Queendom by Lleu's side. The electrifying meeting between Herself and Gronw. Her punishing transformation. As complex as any Celtic Goddess: Is She innocent? Victimized? Marginalized? Adulterous? Betraying? Manipulating? Emancipating?

There are many aspects through which to approach Blodeuwedd. In many ways She stands as a symbol for the journey of women throughout history, and particularly in the mid-20th century, from Object to Subject. The story of Her journey from Lleu's wife to a woman who finds Her own voice and chooses Her passion can be seen as a reflection of the collective journey of women from pre-50's stereotypical roles to post 60's sexual revolutionary freedoms. Far from being the Betrayer, instead She embodies the courage of the risk involved in looking a minimizing situation in the eye and embarking on a course of action that will allow Her Spirit to thrive rather than just survive. Much as the courageous women in the post-WWII era, having had a taste of working outside the home when called to for the war effort, found they could not accept being shoehorned back into previous roles. The result being, not only a shift in social dynamics, but a change in the very way we look at history and approach the future. Women's studies, women's spirituality, equal rights and sexual self-determination all came forth out of the refusal to 'step backwards' into life as it has previously been known.

For Blodeuwedd, the motivating energy that breaks down the illusion of the life She had been sleepwalking through is that of Passion. The moment of seeing Gronw Pebr gallop through the meadow before Her Castle is a transforming moment as significant as the one that turned Her into an Owl later on in Her tale. Though Her body of flowers had been animated by the Spirit that Math and Gwydion called forth, She truly becomes alive the moment She sees Gronw. And that life-force which She experiences flowing through Her for the very first time expresses itself exquisitely (and frequently) with Gronw through...sex.

In the celebration of the Five Goddesses of Avalon, Blodeuwedd is the only one to show us the path towards becoming women in the full expression of our sexuality. The others teach us many things: of life and relationship, passages and mystery, dignity and ownership, grace and loyalty, independence and self-determination. Blodeuwedd is the only one to truly "get down and dirty with the nasty". She and Gronw can't keep their hands off each other! The days become long ordeals to endure until they can finally get back to each others' bodies in bed at night. The very thought of having to put an end to the Passion of their Union is inconceivable to them. It has changed everything that was known before and there is no going backwards.

Though the 'emancipation of women' has touched all areas of life (granted, there are still many places to grow), sexuality seems to be the one that can still offer a challenge to address. Absolutely, there have been massive inroads in this area through the efforts of those engaged in the sexual revolution of the 1960's, but it is not uncommon at all to still find oneself unexpectedly at the barrier of sexual prejudice, stereotypes, judgements or even embarrassment. As often as we find these barriers erected by others, we can also still find them within ourselves. Old concepts, labels or beliefs that continue to stick like that irritating little piece of cellophane you just can't shake off your finger after opening a package. You think you've got it off, then it floats back again.

One woman I know shared something with me many years ago that I have never forgotten. She was in her twenties during the "bra burning" of the 1960's. She experienced the "shame" of the times in having a child out of wedlock. She has been an active voice for women's equality and in that, she has freely shared her experiences, thoughts and revelations. She is vocal in her community and a prolific, exacting journaller. But, she told me, she realized one day that, though she will write about absolutely anything and everything in her journals, when she noted the sexual activity between herself and her husband, she used a tiny, coded symbol tucked into the top corner of the page! Evidence of the one area she was still not able to openly reveal. It made me wonder: In what ways do we still limit ourselves or close ourselves down to full sexual expression without shame? In what ways does the Madonna/Whore dichotomy still inform our sexual expression? And how does this impact on the expression of ourselves as full, whole, free, self-determined, spiritual women? Encountering Blodeuwedd's myth, I discovered another facet to the questioning: What does Blodeuwedd teach us about being true to one's sexual self?

Passion can be expressed in many forms—not just sexually. However, if there is going to be a challenge in expressing it, this is the domain the discomfort tends to fall. Not as relates to our work nor our hobbies nor our relationships nor our commitment to the Earth, our surroundings, our community. And yet, an ability to express ourselves fully sexually is as vital to our holistic health as physical, emotional or spiritual concerns. In looking at ourselves as whole physical and spiritual beings, how can sexuality be separated from that? Sexual passion itself is a flaming urge towards the peak experience of Union, of losing oneself (or finding oneself) in another. It is not easily swayed or contained by rational thought or reason. This desire to move towards Union is not dissimilar to what is experienced spiritually in opening ourselves in ritual to connection and communion with the Goddess. Feeling the Goddess move around us and through us, touching our lives is a spiritual peak experience. Not that far removed from the essence of what unfolds in sexual union. Two energies coming together and melding together into One. However, sexuality, if not out and out taboo, is still a very delicate topic. It is far easier for us to overflow with descriptives of our last ritual than our last orgasm. And yet, I would bet that the language would be very similar!

Blodeuwedd opens us up to the topic of Passion and sexual expression. She is brought to life by the 'other', by Gronw. The touch of that Passion changes everything. What would She say about Her experience? What would Her descriptives be?

"That man touches me and I feel my limbs become fluid. All I want is to sink into him and onto him and have his heat enflame my core" ???

"His hands moving across my body open every tiny bud until I am awash in a sea of nectar" ???

"When our mouths meet, I am the running deer and the soaring hawk, my pulse racing with every brush of his teeth" ???

If we can allow ourselves to spend some time in the week of passionate exchange between Blodeuwedd and Gronw, before moving through to the deception and the Spear and the Owl, how can it help us to deepen our experience of passion and our sexual selves?

As with other areas of spiritual life, I believe that each of the Elements can help us uncover a deeper understanding of this aspect of ourselves.

What of Earth? Opening up to the purely physical experience of sexuality, it is important to know ourselves as well here as in other areas in our lives. Our likes and dislikes, preferences and challenges. To know how we love to be touched. What makes us feel good. What doesn't. If this is to be something we want to communicate to another, we need to know how to put it into words or translate the experience. In some cases, we become so accustomed to accepting how another wants to touch us, we forget that there are preferences that we may have ourselves. If you were to hold and stroke one hand first the way your body is used to being touched and then how you would want your body to be touched, would there be a difference? How would you put that difference into words?

Often when we think of the body sexually, we think of the sexual areas of our body. However, as we are whole sexual beings, our entire body is, in fact an element of sexual expression. Every part of us from our hair down to our toes. Do we engage our whole bodies in our experiences or are there parts we'd rather leave out? Are there any areas of our bodies that we avoid or dislike? Do we see our entire body as sexual or just those parts that have been 'designated' as our sexual bits? What about an elbow or a chin? If there are any parts of your body which you tend to criticize, take a moment to gently touch it. As you move your fingers along that part of yourself, allow yourself to feel the nerves come alive with pleasure. That part too, even if you do not like the look of it, that part too is alive to experience. Imagine your nose feeling left out of a sexual encounter. Or your arms. Or your breasts. When we dislike or even hate a part of our own body, how can we embrace it when we feel most open and vulnerable?

In a broader sense, sexuality opens the door to sensuality - a way of connecting to the world through our physical selves and our senses. That a smell or a taste can awaken us and set our nerves a-tingle. Having this exquisite connection with our own bodies opens us up to an exquisite sensual relationship with the world around us, thus deepening our spiritual connection. A wonderful resource for exploring our relationship with our own bodies, designed for use with a partner, but definitely useful on one's own is *The Art of Sexual Ecstacy* by Margo Anand. Focused on Eastern Tantric and Taoist practices, this book approaches the body and sexual expression from all areas of physical experience, encompassing the senses and how they impact on the raising of energy in us. It is not about achieving an orgasm, but about allowing the full flower of the "awakening the Inner Lover". Experiencing our bodies in this way absolutely changes how we experience the physical world around us. The "Inner Lover" is one in love with the world. It starts with ourselves and emanates outwards in a gorgeous glowing spirals that enlivens all it touches.

Blodeuwedd's message through Earth is: love your Body! It is made of flowers just as surely as Hers is.

What of Water? The first revelation of Passion connected intimately with Blodeuwedd came to me in Imram as the rise, crest and break of an ocean wave. That Passion itself is an energy that ebbs and flows, rising up to a dizzying height before releasing its energy to the Earth. This is a necessary flow, as the intensity of Passion would ultimately be draining to maintain at its height. But, as an energy that electrifies and animates the Soul, it is a vital energy to connect to. This can be a scary thing in the realm of sexuality. By its very nature it breaks down boundaries and barriers, moving us into the realm of altered state experience and leaving us open and exposed. If we experience this in a safe, supported and respectful exchange, it can be a beautifully revelatory experience. If not, it can be the most devastating.

Being aware of the emotions that flood through us in the realm of a sexual experience is imperative. We accept that certain emotions of love and trust will be present, but what of other emotions? Do we experience fear? Resistance to letting down our guard? Is shame present? All of these are like huge boulders in the path of the wave of passion, impeding the flow.

One of the greatest barriers to allowing a healthy emotional connection to sexual energy is having been sexually abused. As Statistics state that 1 in 3 girls have been sexually interfered with (1 in 10 have been incested!), that touches a horrifically large group of women! No wonder many of us experience challenges to our sexual expression. Without question, sexual abuse is the most devastating form of abuse there is. Its impact and repercussions are far deeper and last longer than the results of physical or emotional abuse. This form of abuse cuts to the core of who we are and decimates our ability to trust and be open to others. It tears down a guileless connection with the world around us and replaces it with shame. It tampers with our experience of ourselves, how we see ourselves, how we love ourselves.

It is important to recognize that sexual abuse may not just take the form of nonconsensual touch or penetration. There are many levels to sexual abuse: being looked at in a way that makes you uncomfortable, being exposed to sexual language or images at a young age. There is even a term called "cross-generational bonding", an example being a girl who has replaced the mom in her dad's attention and emotional intimacy. There may be nothing overtly sexual about the relationship, but the relationship dynamic has connected along inappropriate lines, forcing the girl to unconsciously 'grow up' beyond her natural maturity level. Another significant area of trauma may not even be the abusive act itself, but the response to the revelation of the abuse. How authorities have responded, be they parents, police or doctors. A girl or woman who has been sexually abused who must undergo a medical physical within 24 hours of the abuse in order to determine the extent of harm may experience the 'care and concern' as further violation and abuse. As there are degrees to levels of abuse, there are levels to the long-reaching impact and inner negative messages. Without question, sexual abuse involving penetration results in the highest degree of lasting negative impact and emotional interference. However, it is important to recognize that there are many seemingly less traumatic disturbances that may create an inner disconnect with one's sexuality.

There is one key to healing sexual abuse and it can take many, many forms of approach: we must learn not to define ourselves by the actions of our abusers and learn to love and accept ourselves once again. The act of abuse immediately turns us from the Subject of our own life to the Object of another's. To continue to experience shame around the act of the abuse, is to continue to identify as the Object of another. Statistics state that 90% of sex-trade workers have been sexually abused! It is no easy task to reclaim the ownership of our own lives. When the pleasure of our bodies has been used for another's gain or power, how can we embrace our bodies for our own pleasure?

Being aware of any negative emotions we hold in our bodies in response to sexuality is important. The experience of Passion, of Union with another will be challenging, if not impossible, if mistrust, fear and shame are present in our experience. For those who have experienced abuse, *The Courage to Heal* by Ellen Bass and Laura Davis is a phenomenal resource. Covering all areas from impact of abuse to healing from abuse to considerations around confronting the abuser, it offers a doorway through the painful, limiting, negative and debilitating feelings that result from abuse through to a life of choice and intimacy. Though the particular focus of the book is recovering from child sexual abuse, there is so much brilliant information in it about honouring feelings and memories, open and honest communication, involving partners in the healing process, it is extremely beneficial to any woman who finds herself experiencing barriers to allowing trust and openness in sexual expression. I can't recommend it highly enough!

There is no more shame in experiencing our body's pleasure than there is in breathing or laughing or dancing. Our bodies are hard-wired for pleasure. That's why we have a gazillion nerve endings and a wonderful thing known as the clitoris. But it is about our pleasure, our bodies, our experience, our feelings. We are the Subjects in our own Life Story. We are not there to serve as someone else's Object.

A man once tried to cross the sexual line with my sexually symbolic note inscribing friend. One night when she was alone in the house, the phone rang. When she picked it up, there was heavy breathing and much sexually explicit language on the other end of the line. This man had decided that my friend was going to be the Object in his sexual experience. My friend, on the other hand, did not feel threatened and was in fact, somewhat interested and curious. And so she started. With the questions. "So why do you decide to make obscene phone calls? Is it just being bored one night? Are you making your dinner and think "Hey I think I'll obscene phone call someone tonight"? How did you choose me? Do you flip through the phone book?" Very quickly the heavy breathing stopped. The explicit language stopped. And finally the voice on the other end of the line said "Look, lady, I have to go".

Blodeuwedd's message through Water is: love your Self! Pleasure is the soft rain that urges the flowers to bloom.

What of Air? Much of what impacts on our feelings about our sexuality is fed by our beliefs and thoughts about sexuality. Delving into the watery area of our emotions and the earthy experience of our bodies will no doubt quickly reveal our belief system around sex and sexual expression. The deeper we explore those areas, the more the beliefs hidden in the deep recesses of our unconscious will be brought to Light. Many of these beliefs will no doubt be connected to our own experiences, but it is here more than anywhere else that we will find ourselves mired in the cultural muck of sexual shame and mixed messages. What is 'normal'? What is not? What is 'okay'? What is not? How do I respond to terms like 'prude', 'frigid', 'slut', 'whore'? How do I react to thoughts of sexual activity at the age of 14? 24? 34? 44? 54? 64? 74? 84??? If we, as parents, have sex with our partners and we feel okay about that, why is it still so uncomfortable to think about our parents having sex?

I have always wished I had the courage to talk to my Mom, woman to woman about her sexual experiences. I know almost everything about how she experienced the changing roles of women through the decades of the 20th century. Born in 1923, she saw a world that radically changed for women through her lifetime. And she was very much a part of that change. But I never knew how it affected her sexually or in her attitudes toward sex, other than what I could discern by reading between the lines. In fairness, interestingly, I believe this barrier to communication came from me. I will never forget one exchange, sitting in a coffeeshop with her, after the dissolution of a very bad relationship. We chattered about life's events for a bit, then fell silent with our thoughts. After a moment, she looked me in the eye and said: "I haven't been able to figure out why you stayed in that relationship. The only thing I can think is that he must have been really good in bed". My Goddess! From my mother! I did manage to sputter a response, but that was the end of the conversation. A lost opportunity. One belief system I was not able to release in that moment. The same barrier that arose when she asked me once what "oral sex" was and I had the same sputtery response, referring her to her knowledge of Latin.

There are inner places we are not able to go beyond and that is okay. But, as with other areas in our lives, if we don't know where those barriers come up, we don't have choice as to whether we want them there or not.

In doing research for a workshop on 'the masks women wear', I was presented with a pornographic video of a woman in her 80's. I found it very challenging to watch. The images doing more to push against beliefs I didn't realize I had than any amount of reading on the subject could do. What was extraordinary about this video was that the director interviewed the woman after the act, asking her why she agreed to do the video. She responded "Because everyone thinks that once you reach a certain age, sex is off limits. I wanted to show people that you never stop being a sexual person. No matter what age, it is a part of who we are." She was amazingly composed, self-possessed and not an iota of shame. She was a revelation.

For those who have not watched the HBO series "Sex and the City", it offers an opportunity to explore some of the beliefs which tend to be prevalent in our society today. Of course, it is solely based on the perspective of 30-something single urban women which by necessity puts certain limitations around what is being explored. But, as a forum which exists in our current pop culture through which to be exposed to some ideas around: when to have sex, what is 'normal' or not in sex, how does having sex change things in a relationship, what is the role of passion in sex, marriage and sex, the impact of having children on having sex etc, etc., it is the most comprehensive and entertaining that I have come across so far.

Here's an exercise: watch an episode of "Sex and the City". Allow yourself to feel that you are open-minded and modern in your views on sex and sexuality. Then, at the part when one of the women is in the midst of passionate union with her current lover, have your father come into the room, take a glance at the tv and say "What in the world are you watching?". Notice how all your "open-minded and modern" self-perceptions shrivel and plop on the floor as you quickly mutter "it's a very popular tv show" and scurry to turn off the tv. This is an excellent way of exposing inner barriers. I know. I tried it.

One thing that is wonderful about "Sex and the City" is that, to the extent that it can be done on television, it promotes the courage of asking the questions (exploring what we believe about sex and where we may be challenged in our beliefs) without the devastating paralysis that can be wrought with the presence of shame. We need to have beliefs. They help us to emanate the particular flavour that is our unique Essence. But to have beliefs that are informed by shame gives us the message that there is something wrong with who we are. Shame does not protect Essence. It cuts us off from Essence. Choice illuminates Essence. To explore our beliefs around sexuality, release those beliefs that are held in place by shame and replace them with beliefs that we choose as being reflective of who we is as empowering as Blodeuwedd taking Gronw to Her bed.

Blodeuwedd's message through Air is: know your Self! Nurturing the roots of affirming beliefs blossoms forth flowers of vibrant beauty.

What of Fire? Ah! Fire! The very heart and heat of Passion. Having explored our bodies, our emotions, our beliefs, what is left to explore? Our fantasies! And if this isn't tricky ground, I don't know what is.

Even in the closest of female friendships where an openness to share one's sexual explorations and questions is firmly established, often a line is drawn at being able to reveal the fantasies that dance through our most private visions. Very often, in allowing our minds to range free, some of the visions that appear behind our eyes are ones we can barely acknowledge to ourselves. Our sexual fantasies are the most sensitive, closely guarded secrets we have. But, again, it is important to distinguish between privacy and secrecy. Wanting to keep our visions close because we want to honour their special relationship to our sexual life is wonderful. Wanting to be very particular about who we share the language of our fantasies with is acknowledging the trust within certain relationships we have. But to close our fantasies off behind a wall of secrecy because we fear what judgements may be leveled against us brings us back into the painful and destructive realm of shame.

In 1973, a very courageous woman wrote a book called *My Secret Garden*. Nancy Friday, a journalist, compiled interviews with women discussing and sharing details of their innermost sexual fantasies. Never before had such a book hit the stands and it was a sensation. The most common response being: "Oh thank God, I'm not the only one!"

Just as dreams offer us insight into our unconscious and meditations offer us insight into our higher guidance, fantasies offer us insight into our particular unique sexual language. The problem with fantasy can be that we mistake having a vision with wanting that vision to recreate and manifest itself in our lives. The most common fantasy for women to have is 'the rape fantasy'. Does this mean that most women secretly desire being raped? Absolutely not! As with dream language, there is something deeper going on. Rape fantasies have more to do with being able to explore depths of passionate sexual expression without fear of falling into the tarpit of slutty recriminations than they have to do being sexually overpowered. Rape is about violence. Rape fantasies are about freedom to experience without risk of shame. We would no more want that fantasy to occur in our day-to-day life than we would want some of our dream imagery to occur. We may fantasize about a steamy afternoon tryst with the milkman (so to speak), but does this mean that we really want the cold water bucket of reality of seeing him again the next day in our ratty nightgown or throwing the relationship that we have spent years of care and attention to into crisis. Again, absolutely not! Although, to bring balance to this, if you want to dress in a micro mini skirt and stilettos to share an adventure in a safe, supportive sexual environment with a loved one, what harm in that? You wouldn't wear it to work, perhaps, but it certainly allows for a different experience of oneself.

Fantasies breathe life into our sexual experience. They are not there to serve the purpose of shaming us or punishing us. If we are truly connected to the health, vitality and affirmation of our sexual life, fantasies are a major key in unlocking the door to Passion.

Blodeuwedd's message through Fire is: honour your Visions! The Passion that is sparked alights us as surely as a summer sun on a flower's beauty.

What of Spirit? Moving through each of these Elements and bringing their distinct voices to our sexual experience can no doubt result in the balance necessary to achieve that Fifth Element: the Element of Spiritual Balance, the Divine. Indeed the Goddess Herself experienced within and without in all aspects of our physical, emotional and mental selves. In our lives and in our Spirits, we are women open to bringing Passion into our experiences. With our whole selves, we reach out and touch the Goddess. Could it be described thus?

She touches me and I feel my limbs become fluid. All I want is to sink into the energy of the Goddess and allow Her heat to enflame my core.

The Goddess' energy moves across my body, opening every tiny bud until I am awash in a sea of nectar.

In the energy of the Goddess, I am the running deer and the soaring hawk, my pulse racing.

I would suggest that sexuality is as imperative to spiritual expression as energy work, ritual, knowledge of Universal laws. I would suggest that Blodweuwedd is a key Goddess to opening up our experience of sexuality and allowing an inner dialogue of sexual experience to occur. The Goddess Blodeuwedd, in Her discovery of Her passionate, sexual Self gives us permission to allow our own bodies to come alive with the acceptance of a body's desire, the thrill of Passion and the ecstatic union with another. And as we deepen the experience of union with Self, it can't help but impact on our experience of union with our lovers and our experience of Union with the Divine. Passion is the same current of energy and intimacy is the same expression of trust—no matter which direction it flows.

Like Blodeuwedd, we are flowers in the Universe of our experience. Through Her, I have begun to see the receptivity of our bodies to sensuality as the budding of a flower in Spring, the strength of our passion as the wave of blossoming and the ecstatic experience of an orgasm, the cresting of all our senses brought together in a moment of fluid release, as the gorgeous bloom of a flower in full, sharing its beauty with the world all around it. What a gift She offers us!

> In the white glow of Passion's embrace
> The Goddess sighs Her electric charge
> By the Earth that is Her Glory
> By the Water of Her Orgasmic Touch
> By the Air of Her Acceptance
> By the Fire of Her Surging Clutch
> The bud sings towards the Stars.
> In the single sweep of a petal's curve
> They pause to inhale
> Passionflower.
> And the Universe
> waltzes,
> jigs,
> boogies,
> and steamy salsas
> on.

RESOURCES

Anand, Margo, T*he Art of Sexual Ecstasy: The Path of Sacred Sexuality for Western Lovers* (G.P. Putnam's Sons), 1989.

Anand, Margo, *The Art of Everyday Ecstacy* (Broadway), 1999.

Anand, Margo, *Sexual Ecstasy: The Art of the Orgasm* (Tarcher), 2000.

Bass, Ellen and Davis, Laura, *The Courage to Heal: A Guide for Women Survivors of Child Sexual Abuse* (Harper & Row), 1988.

Bass, Ellen and Davis, Laura, *Beginning to Heal: A First Book for Survivors of Child Abuse* (Perennial), 1993.

Bass, Ellen, *I Never Told Anyone: Writings by Women Survivors of Child Sexual Abuse* (Harper Paperbacks), 1991.

Forward, Susan, *Betrayal of Innocence: Incest and Its Devastation* (Penquin), 1988.

Friday, Nancy, *My Secret Garden*, Trident Press 1973, (reissued by Simon and Schuster), 2008.

Friday, Nancy, *Forbidden Flowers* (Simon and Schuster), 1991.

Friday, Nancy, *Women on Top*, (Simon and Schuster), 1993.

Other Media

Not a Love Story: A Film about Pornography
Director: Bonnie Sherr Klein
National Film Board of Canada
1985
(for more information, visit www.nfb.ca)

Sex and the City
HBO Television series

Midday Prayer to Blodeuwedd

BY JULIE BOND

O Blodeuwedd,
Maid of flowers, the Oak, the Broom, and the Meadowsweet;
Lady called forth by Math and Gwydion,
I greet you this noon-tide.
At the centre of the year the Oak flowers bloom,
Watching over the magic of Midsummer Night.
O Blodeuwedd,
with strength you chose your own path,
Please guide me in choices on mine.
O Blodeuwedd, Flower-Face,
O Lady who made your own choice;
As blossoms garland the land
and all Nature blooms forth,
I honour you this Noon and this Spring.

Llyn Morwynion (The Lake of the Maidens) - In an attempt to escape the wrath of Gwydion for her betrayal of Lleu, Bloduewedd and her ladies fled their court in search of safety; however, save for Blodeuwedd, all of the women fell into the lake which now bears their name and drowned because they kept looking behind them in fear of their pursuer.

PHOTO CREDIT: JHENAH TELYNDRU

Hanes Blodeuwedd

Jhenah Telyndru

Words and Music by Jhenah Telyndru © 1992. All rights reserved.

Animal Encounters on the Spiral Path: Owls

A Retelling of the Story of Blodeuwedd and the Origin of Owls

BY SHARON CROWELL-DAVIS

Blodeuwedd's breath came in quick gasps as she struggled up the faint path left by the sturdy mountain sheep. Her shoes and the hem of her robe were soaked with water from the edges of bogs that she and her companions had stumbled into. Behind her was Gwydion and a horde of mounted men. Gwydion had changed her life forever when he gathered together a host of flowers, flowers that should have finished blossoming and formed seeds to create more flowers to fill the land with bright color and sweet scent, and used their life force to make the body of a human maiden. Having done that, he presumed that he could tell her who to lie with and who to love.

Gwydion had not understood that, once the body of a maiden is formed, and the soul of a maiden called into it, she was her own self. She was not a thing to be owned, but a woman with her own choices to make. So it had come to pass that, instead of loving Llew Llaw Gyffes, his nephew, the man for whom Gwydion had made her and who acted like he owned her, she had come to love Gronw. Gronw was kind to her, listened to her, cared about her and, most importantly, loved her. She had not been able to speak around Llew, for he did not want to hear her thoughts. He had only wanted to enjoy the touch of her body. In her sadness at the plight she had found herself in, she had wandered into the apple orchard, and sat amongst the flowers that she had once been one of. There Gronw found her and asked her what troubled her. He sat and listened, and eventually told her of his own heart, and so they had come to love each other.

That beautiful afternoon, sitting among the flowers in the apple orchard, with apple blossoms drifting in the air and falling into their hair, would forever be a precious memory for Blodeuwedd. They had become lovers, secretive in their trysts as they should not have had to be. Other women chose whom they could love and marry. Why couldn't Blodeuwedd? She couldn't because Gwydion said she was for Llew. She couldn't because Llew said she belonged to him. Eventually, to free her, Gronw had killed Llew. For a while they were happy together. But now Gwydion and his uncle, Math, had brought armies against them. So Blodeuwedd and the maidens who had become her friends had fled into the mountains while Gronw prepared the men loyal to him to fight the armies of Math and Gwydion, hoping that he could keep them occupied while she escaped into hiding.

However, that had not happened. She had defied Gwydion's commands that she be obedient to Llew, and his wrath was as much with her as it was with Gronw. So while the standard of Math and the horsemen following it had headed toward the stronghold where Gronw waited, the standard of Gwydion and some other riders had paused for a while, then continued up into the mountains, following the trail of Blodeuwedd. The breath of all the maidens came short, and they were dizzy with the long running, constantly looking back, occasionally catching glimpses through the curves of the mountainsides of the horsemen coming ever closer.

For a moment, Blodeuwedd paused to catch her breath, looking back to see if she could discern how much the wrathful Gwydion had closed the distance between them. Then she heard a series of screams and shrieks behind her. She turned and saw that all her friends were gone, disappeared as if the wind had grabbed them and, all in a rush, taken them away to some distant land. Trembling with fear, she walked the few feet of trail to where they had been but a moment ago. Then she saw. The trail did not reach the top of the crest, then bend downward, following the curve of a mountain slope. The trail ended at a cliff, a long, bare wall of harsh stone. At the bottom lay her friends, still and quiet. Blodeuwedd looked around. To the left, the ground fell away steeply, ending in a sheep path that would likely converge with the path that Gwydion and his men were on even now. To the right, the path rose steeply for a short distance, then seemed to disappear on a hilltop. Blodeuwedd turned right and carefully walked 30 steps to the top. There, she found herself on a high promontory. On three sides, the grassy earth fell away steeply, to lower land where Gwydion would eventually find her. On the fourth side, the land still fell away sharply, a cold, cruel cliff, the cliff that had taken the lives of her friends.

Blodeuwedd held back tears, wished Gwydion had left her as flowers, to form seeds that would fall into the earth, to grow and bloom and form more flowers. But he hadn't. He had changed her into a woman and, instead of letting her live as a woman, had commanded her to be a thing, a warm, soft thing for his nephew to lie with. In her short time as a maiden, Blodeuwedd had known much pain, but she had also known much love. Gronw's love had shown her the best that men could be. While he enjoyed the pleasures of the body that came when he lay with her, as she had enjoyed lying with him, he had also shown her love and tenderness and consideration. He had put thought to her happiness, and not just the satisfaction of his own lust as Llew had. The five maidens who had befriended her had taught her the love and friendship of women. They had been like sisters, even though Blodeuwedd had been made from flowers and her friends had been born of the bodies of five different women. All of that was ended now.

Standing on that high precipice, Blodeuwedd felt the winds blow her tears away. Far below she heard a shout. Gwydion's men had spotted her and even now urged their horses up the steep mountainside. What should she do? Should she attempt to run further, down the mountainside farthest from them? No, she could run and run and run and they would eventually catch her. Then they would kill her or worse, force her into bondage with some other man of Gwydion's choice, as humiliation and punishment for daring to love whom she chose. Should she jump off the cliff and join her friends? A part of her said to do that, but another part railed against such a fate. She had been a human maiden for only a few short months. She wanted to live. It was evening and the full moon had just risen above the eastern horizon. From her vantage on the mountaintop Blodeuwedd could see it earlier than most. She thought of the one who, ultimately, had made her even though the magician Gwydion had reformed her.

"Goddess, you made me, as you made all life. Gwydion has warped my form and forbidden my love. Please, please, if you will, give me another form. Let me love as I will."

Then she put her face in her hands and waited for what would happen. As the evening wind blew up the cliff, blowing Blodeuwedd's long hair skyward, the sun set and the moon rose and the dark shadows of twilight passed across the land. Gwydion and his men closed the distance that separated them from Blodeuwedd. Her hands came away from her face and she raised them beside the flowing mass of her hair. Arms turned into wings. Hair turned into feathers. Her body turned into the body of a bird. Blodeuwedd rose, coasted on the rising wind in the darkening sky, and launched herself off the cliff top. She did not fall. Instead, she rose high on the winds for a time, coasting in the darkening skies far away, to a forest where Gwydion would not find her.

Gwydion, arriving foremost among his men, pulled his horse up in a startled rear. It fell over backwards, casting Gwydion upon the ground. He rose and staggered to the top of the mountain again. There was no sign of Blodeuwedd, who had been there moments before. His horse had broken its neck in the sudden fall and he had injured his ankle. He swore and spat curses into the wind but the wind carried them away so that they came to nothing. He was thwarted.

Darkness had fallen on the battlefield where Gronw and his men fought the soldiers of Math. Many were dead but Gronw still stood, though he was sorely wounded. Men were becoming hesitant to fight in the growing darkness. The sun had set and though the full moon would soon bring more light, it was not high enough yet to do so. So in that moment when day is gone and night has not truly started, in that moment when the way is open between the worlds, Gronw suddenly found himself to be, not a man, but a bird and free of wounds as well. Goddess sent a heavy mist up from a nearby pond, and the surrounding bogs, and blinded Math and his men, as well as the men of Gronw, so that the fighting utterly stopped. In that fog, the bird that was Gronw took wing, for he could suddenly see better than the humans around him and his hearing was so acute that he could detect and identify the subtlest of movements around him. He flew into the forest and hid there for many days.

Over time, the bird that was Gronw felt a pull to travel in a certain direction. Always he traveled by night, watching for small creatures disturbing the leaves as he did so. When this happened he dove and grabbed them in his talons. Then, feeling a sense of urgency to keep moving, he consumed them whole. During the day when the sun shone high in the sky, the men of Math and Gwydion still searched for the missing Gronw, hoping they might find him. He rested, clutching branches close to the trunks of trees, camouflaged by the many shades of brown that formed his plumage. For many days he traveled until he was beyond the lands ruled by Math and his kin.

Then one night he spotted a small mouse rustling in the leaves. Quickly, he dove after it but another bird stooped even as he did, grabbing the mouse and winging its way up to a nearby tree branch. Angry, he followed the bird. Landing beside it, he intended to fight the other bird for possession of the mouse. The other bird looked at him. Then they recognized each other. Blodeuwedd and Gronw were reunited. Bending his head in deference, Gronw stepped back, acknowledging that the mouse belonged to Blodeuwedd, his love.

In the coming months and years, Blodeuwedd and Gronw raised many clutches of young. So it was that they were the parents of the race of birds that humans call owls. They hunt at night, keen-eyed and keen-eared in the darkness that humans fear. A mated pair, like Blodeuwedd and Gronw, remain loyal to each other for life.

More About Owls

Over 200 species of owls inhabit the earth, existing on all continents except Antarctica. Ranging in size from the 6 inch long Elf Owl that weighs 40 grams (1.3 oz) to the 28 inch long Eurasian Eagle Owl that weighs 4200 grams (9 pounds), owls are birds of prey that hunt primarily at night. They can see during daylight hours about as well as most birds but have exceptional night vision. Their eyes are prominently on the front of their face and a distinct formation of feathers, called the "face plate", funnels sounds into their ears. These feathers produce the unique and distinctive faces of owls, and doubtless contributed to the naming of the heroine Goddess Blodeuwedd, whose name in Welsh means "Flower Face". Owls rely on their keen hearing, as well as their excellent night vision, to hunt during the night.

Owls have been present in the stories and art of humans for millennia. In various parts of the world owls have been revered and respected, while in others they have been considered harbingers of death and creatures to be dreaded. Owls are long-lived birds, with banded individuals of some species approaching 30 years of age. This may have contributed to the concept of the owl being "wise" that is common in western culture.

Owls are like most animals in that the females are larger than the males. This size differential probably serves several functions. The larger female stays with the eggs and the young to brood and guard them, while the male hunts and brings food back to her. The great majority of owls exhibit total fidelity throughout the breeding and chick-rearing season and in many species a pair will remain together for life.

In the story of Blodeuwedd that is presented in The Mabinogion, she is simply referred to as turning into "an owl". This leaves the question of which kind of owl she might have been turned into. The Common Barn Owl, *Tyto alba*, is a likely candidate. It lives in temperate and warm climates throughout the world, including much of Europe, all of the British Isles and Ireland, and North America up to approximately the border between the United States and Canada. The Barn Owl avoids areas that have more than 1 to 2 months of continuous snow cover. The female and male Barn Owl mate for life, with the breeding season of each year starting with an elaborate aerial courtship.

The Long-eared Owl, *Asio otus*, is also dispersed throughout wide regions of the world including: Great Britain, Ireland, much of Continental Europe, and North America, although its range extends farther north than does that of the Barn Owl. Its name derives from prominent tufts of feathers that are not ears. Because the feather tufts covering the ears of the Long-eared owl are such a prominent aspect of its appearance, it does not seem likely that this is the owl of the Blodeuwedd story. The long feather-tufts, likened to horns in some cultures, would probably have been included in the story. The Short-eared Owl, *Asio flammeus*, gets its name from the lack of long feather tufts covering its ears. Its range is similar to, but more extensive than, the Long-eared Owl and it is possible that Blodeuwedd was based on the attractive face of this species.

The Tawny Owl, *Strix aluco*, is the one owl species that probably existed in Wales at the time the stories of the Mabinogion originated but did not exist anywhere in the Americas. It has an extensive range in Europe and Southeastern Asia and likewise may have been the basis for the owl of the story of Blodeuwedd.

While we can never know with certainty which owl species the owl of the story of Blodeuwedd is based upon, I like to think of the owl more generically. In the patriarchal society in which her story was written down, long after it had originated, women were perceived as property, owing total fidelity to whatever man they were given to. Thus, she is portrayed as an unfaithful wife and an adulteress. However, in the more ancient Celtic society, women were active participants in the decision of whom they would marry. So the part of the story portraying her as an unfaithful wife is in error. Gwydion, Math and Llew treated her as a slave; to use modern parlance, she was a sex slave. She had to use wisdom, cunning and boldness to escape from the man who had enslaved her. Here, her ultimate conversion to an owl is consistent. Owls are long-lived and have a reputation for wisdom and cunning derived, in part, from what skillful hunters they are during the night when humans do not function well in the woods. Finally, ultimately, I see her story as one of fidelity and loyalty. Just as owls mate for life, Blodeuwedd, having chosen her mate, chose him for life. Ultimately, the hidden story is a love story, and not a story of betrayal.

REFERENCES

Duncan, James R., *Owls of the world: their lives, behavior and survival* (Firefly Books), 2003.

Photo by Sharon Crowell-Davis

Blodeuwedd Beside Me

BY ELISA

From winter's chill
You emerge
In verdant hue
Maiden Fair

From soft slumber
You rouse me
And place feathers
In my hair

With morning's dew
You crown me
And breaking long—
Winter's grip

Stand beside me
Hands as chalice
Holy water
To my lips

Queen Blodeuwedd
Flower Face
Looks upon me,
Draws me near

Summons beauty
Springtime's songs
Whispering change
In my ear

Blodeuwedd (Wisdom of Owl)

Adara Bryn

Words and Music by Adara Bryn © 2015. All rights reserved.

Blodeuwedd's Charge

BY KELLY WOO

I am the Spring time air—a crisp breeze that awakens and invigorates the senses with a hint of warmth that teases like an enticing kiss, promising adventurous days and passionate nights.

I am the waxing moon and the rising sun, swelling with infinite possibility, mysterious and wonderful.

Created from the beauty and grace of nine flowers, I am She who has been called Flower Face. But let not my name fool you, for I radiate strength and conviction.

Like a stirring song, I call to your soul.

Tell me your secret desires and I will help make them manifest, for I am dreams made flesh.

Let my light fill the darkest corners of your self and illuminate that which has been hidden, bringing understanding and healing.

Cast aside expectation and find the courage that resides within that you may rise above, unshackled and free.

For I am also the Owl Maiden, whose swift wings lift you to such great heights.

They banished me to the solitude of night, yet my keen sight pierces the darkness and brings clarity. In the silence of the soul, I know myself. I am free and this gift of self-knowledge I offer you.

Rise with me.

Emerge renewed.

Blodeuwedd's Gift

BY ROBIN CORAK

*P*ay attention to your breathing. When you are ready, you step through a door and over a threshold into a beautiful land. A beautiful young woman radiating a vibrant golden light greets you and motions for you to follow her.

You notice that spring has just begun in this land, but something does not feel right. You feel a slight breeze and pull your dull, lightweight black cloak closer to your body. As you survey the land you see plants on the verge of blooming, you sense the seeds of life poised to push their way through the soil and make their presence known, but for some reason everything seems frozen, stilted, as if held back from what could be. Your ask your guide's name. She smiles innocently and answers simply, "Blodeuwedd".

You look over Blodeuwedd's shoulder and see that she is leading you to what appears to be a great labyrinth in the very center of the land. You notice a fine, almost invisible mist creating a threshold over which you must cross to enter the labyrinth. As you approach the threshold, Blodeuwedd speaks.

"Every living being has the ability to reach its highest, greatest potential. We are born without limits, and yet we women in particular allow ourselves to be defined by others in so many ways. We strive to nurture and please others, to fulfill their vision of us, and by doing so it is not uncommon for us to sacrifice ourselves. To become stagnant, frozen, forever poised on the threshold of potential and manifestation. As you travel through to the core of this labyrinth, making the many twists and turns, I ask that you travel deep within as well. I ask that you identify the many parts you feel compelled to play, the labels you wear which are imposed upon you by others, society, even yourself. Dwell within each of them, explore them, let them settle over you like a mantle, just as you have inhabited their energy in your mundane life. I implore you to think well about how these labels imposed upon you by others have held you from reaching your highest potential, and perhaps, how they have dishonored and shamed you or caused you pain."

With great trepidation you look towards the labyrinth. You are not sure that you are strong enough to do this. You are not sure that you want to do this, but as you glance back at Blodeuwedd, she whispers, "I will be here waiting for you." Something in her eyes gives you the strength that you need to move forward.

As you begin walking the labyrinth, you start with the simple labels and expectations that others have used to define who you are and/or should be as a mother, a partner, a friend. As you name each label and explore its meanings and implications, you have the strangest sensation, as though someone were enfolding you in another layer of clothing. The mists thicken into a soupy fog as you continue to travel your path, deep into the core of the labyrinth. As you continue your introspection, you find that identifying the labels and what they mean to you is becoming harder, more intimidating, and with the naming of each label, another cloak is draped over your shoulders until you find yourself hunched over with the weight of the excess baggage you carry. The sky is no longer plagued by fog, for now the grey mists have slowly turned to the thick, inky black of night and you strain to make out your next steps.

A part of you—a shadow within you perhaps—begs and screams, pleading for you to stop the slow excavation of the limitations, personas, and beliefs you have allowed others to place upon you. Despite your fears, despite your weariness, you trod forward, digging deeper and deeper as you get closer to the labyrinth's center. Finally, when you think that you cannot bear to take another step, you approach the opening of a cave. You step in, hoping to find solace, but the interior of the cave does not feel comforting. You can barely make out before you a pool of water, ever so slightly illuminated by the thin waxing moon overhead. With great effort, you stoop to drink from the pool and to splash your face with the refreshing liquid. As you do so, you catch the briefest glimpse of your figure in the water. You see a woman before you, hunched and burdened by the many dark, shadowy cloaks that coil around her, threatening to suffocate her and preventing her from further movement. You realize that each of these cloaks represents a label or belief you have allowed to be placed upon you, thus wearing you down, chaining you to the shadows that lurk within, limiting your control and power and stunting your ability to evolve and grow.

Shaking, you take a deep breath and struggle to rise to a standing position. You desire nothing more than to free yourself from the burdens you have carried. Slowly but surely you emerge from the cave and begin to journey back out through the labyrinth to your starting point. As you walk, you remove your cloaks one by one, naming them and stating, "I release you, you no longer serve me." At first this takes a great deal of energy and you are so worn out with each effort that you begin to lose faith that you will ever make it out of the labyrinth, but Blodeuwedd's parting words ring in your ears and you find the strength to persevere. Soon you realize that with each cloak you shed, with each label you release, you feel lighter, better able to stand erect. The atmosphere is changing as well so that with each release the air feels less thick and the sky seems to lighten. You can feel the energy, hope, and thrill of freedom returning within you and to the land itself.

With one last step you release your final cloak and are immediately filled with a rush of exhilaration and a confidence, exuberance, power, and belief in endless possibilities that you have not felt in some time—perhaps even since you were a child. You bound over the threshold and into Blodeuwedd's arms, reveling in your newfound strength and faith. Blodeuwedd laughs softly, and leads you to a nearby stream, where you can see a reflection of yourself once again. This time, however, the picture is sharp and clear and you are astonished to find that you are wrapped in nothing but a luminescent, shining light.

For the first time perhaps in many years you do not see your flaws and foibles, but instead, you see the beauty that resides within you and you experience a deep self love, much like the unconditional love of a mother for her child. You turn to Blodeuwedd and before you can express your gratitude, she beckons you to follow her. You watch, awed, as her face transforms into the mask of an owl and her body shifts until the transformation is complete. You feel your body contorting as well until you are looking out at the world through wide, knowing eyes and where the cloaks once rested upon your back there are now wings.

You take flight and follow the goddess as she soars ever higher into the twilight sky. You observe the labyrinth below in wonder and admiration. The sky's color deepens and stars shine brightly against a sapphire canvas. You are not sure why but you feel compelled to weave a beautiful work of art using the stars as your thread and the sky as your loom. As you weave, you think about what you wish to be, what you wish to manifest in your life. You begin to identify new labels—new mantles to wear that better fit your essence, and which will serve you and align you with all that you believe and desire. As you create your vision, the stars twinkle and change colors until you are finally able to observe your finished product and your breath catches at its beauty.

Following Blodeuwedd, you descend to the ground and feel yourself transform back into the woman who emerged from the labyrinth. Blodeuwedd turns to you and hands you a gift stating, "I believe this will serve you and fit you better than what you wore into my world."

You gasp as you unfold the most beautiful, amazing, magical cloak you have ever seen in your life. Beautiful in its intensity, the vivid colors seem to shine and move in an intricate dance. What's more, the cloak is the embodiment of the mosaic you created amongst the stars—a perfect representation of the essence of your highest self. You embrace Blodeuwedd warmly, touched by her gift, and you thank her for her wisdom and love.

Blodeuwedd reminds you that this cloak is yours to wear as a reminder of the potential, power, and beauty that exists within you and the unique gifts which you have to offer the world. She informs you that you may change the cloak whenever you feel it serves you to do so. Finally, she encourages you to adorn yourself in the cloak whenever you begin to feel yourself giving in to the ominous pressure and burden of the heavy, inhibiting cloaks that others would have you wear. Filled with love and awe and a renewed confidence and strength, you once again embrace Blodeuwedd and thank her. Then, you turn and walk towards the door leading to the mundane world from which you came, knowing that you can return to Blodeuwedd and to this magical land should you ever feel the need or desire to do so.

Maid of Flowers, Made of Flowers

BY JHENAH TELYNDRU

he mythic archetype of the Flower Maiden or Flower Bride is a powerful image that likely has its roots in the international folk motif of Sovereignty—a personification of the land with whom a prospective king must mate in order to assume the throne. While this component of her character is not explicitly stated in the Fourth Branch of *Y Mabinogi* where her story is told, Blodeuwedd is brought into being when Arianrhod, the mother of Lleu Llaw Gyffes, lays a *tynged* upon him, forbidding him to marry any woman from the race currently on the earth. Having previously denied Lleu a name and the ability to bear arms unless she herself named or armed him—which she was eventually tricked into doing by her magician brother, Gwydion—Arianrhod's final destiny upon her son appeared to be irresolvable; without a bride, Lleu could neither come into his own as a man, nor ever take his place as a ruler in his own right. Gwydion brought this problem before his uncle Math, an even more powerful magician, and together they conceived of a plan:

> Then they took the flowers of the oak, and the flowers of the broom, and the flowers of the meadowsweet, and from those they conjured up the fairest and most beautiful maiden that anyone had ever seen. And they baptized her, and gave her the name of Blodeuedd.— (Davies, p. 58)

It is interesting that the redactor of the tale was so very specific about the flowers used to create Blodeuwedd. These particular blooms may well have held a significance which would have been immediately understood by the contemporary medieval audience—a significance we can only guess at, but which may well have imparted specific information about the nature of Blodeuwedd's character. The oak is a tree closely associated

96

with the Solar Hero in many cultures, and it is this very tree which houses the wounded Lleu when he is in eagle-form (yet another solar association) later on in the tale. It is, of course, a tree that was sacred to the Celts, and very much associated with the Druids; its inclusion may well reflect a druidic origin of the magics of Math and Gwydion. The broom is used as a descriptor for Olwen's yellow hair in the medieval Welsh tale *Culhwch ac Olwen*, and while it may be mentioned to likewise allude to Blodeuwedd's hair color, it is also a herb used in the *materia medica* of the Physicians of Myddfai—a world-famous Welsh lineage of healers—to cool fevers. Broom was used to cleanse the house on May Day, and was often included in brides' bouquets, as was meadowsweet which is also known by the name "bridewort." Interestingly, meadowsweet has also been used as a funerary herb and perhaps its presence here presages the role Blodeuwedd will play in Lleu's "death."

In addition to folkloric uses, each of these three herbs have medicinal qualities as well. Oak (*Quercus robur*) is a powerful astringent and antiseptic, making it useful to treat wounds, staunch bleeding, and to quell fevers. Its astringent properties are especially helpful in cases of chronic diarrhea, and as a pulling poultice to draw out infection and inflammation. It can be used to ease respiratory infections, to treat hemorrhoids, and has antiviral and antifungal properties.

Broom (*Cytisus scoparius*) is a powerful cleansing herb, both energetically and physically, as it is traditionally used in the making of besoms, as its name suggests; it was also used to weave baskets and to thatch roofs. Its fibers were spun to make cloth, and the tannins in its bark made it useful for tanning leather. This common plant's roots anchor soil, thereby preventing erosion, especially when it grows along the coastline, and its branches shelter wildlife. As a protective herb, it can be burned to dispel negative influences. Broom was famously used in Brittany as a heraldic device, and the English royal house of Plantagenet took the plant's medieval name, *planta genista*, as its own. Medicinally, broom has been used traditionally to treat complaints of the cardiovascular system, as a diuretic, and to induce labor; however, caution should be practiced when taking this herb internally. It should only be used under professional supervision, as poisoning can occur.

Meadowsweet (*Spiraea ulmaria*). Also called "bridewort," the sweet smelling flowers of the meadowsweet are a traditional addition to the bridal bouquet. It is also a common funerary herb, and so perhaps represented the transition from one life phase to the next. According to Grieve, the Druids held meadowsweet in high regard, and counted it as one of their three most sacred herbs, along with vervain and water mint. Said to instill a sense of gladness and peace, meadowsweet flowers were strewn on the floors of houses, and was a popular ingredient in the making of mead and ale. Meadowsweet contains salicylates, the primary component of aspirin, and so has traditional usage for pain relief and the reduction of fevers. Among its many medicinal uses, it is an excellent anti-spasmodic, and assists with menstrual cramps.

In his seminal work, *The White Goddess*, 20th century British author and mythologist Robert Graves deconstructs the story of Blodeuwedd in the context of his theories, and includes a poem called "Hanes Blodeuwedd." It is based in part on "Cad Goddeu" ("The Battle of the Trees"), a poem from the 14th century Welsh manuscript *Llyfr Taliesin* (*The Book of Taliesin*) Peniarth MS 2, which has several lines that appear to refer to the creation of Blodeuwedd by Math and Gwydion:

> When I was made,
> Did my Creator create me.
> Of nine-formed faculties,
> Of the fruit of fruits,
> Of the fruit of the primordial God,
> Of primroses and blossoms of the hill,
> Of the flowers of trees and shrubs.
> Of earth, of an earthly course,
> When I was formed.
> 160 Of the flower of nettles,
> Of the water of the ninth wave.
> I was enchanted by Math,
> Before I became immortal,
> I was enchanted by Gwydyon
> The great purifier of the Brython

Graves appears to have extracted these verses and added to them in the writing of his "Hanes Blodeuwedd" ("The History of Blodeuwedd"):

> Not of father nor of mother
> Was my blood, was my body.
>
> I was spellbound by Gwydion,
> Prime enchanter of the Britons,
> When he formed me from nine blossoms,
> Nine buds of various kind;
> From primrose of the mountain,
> Broom, meadow-sweet and cockle,
> Together intertwined,
> From the bean in its shade bearing
> A white spectral army
> Of earth, of earthly kind,
> From blossoms of the nettle,

Oak, thorn and bashful chestnut—
Nine powers of nine flowers,
Nine powers in me combined,
Nine buds of plant and tree.

Long and white are my fingers
As the ninth wave of the sea.

We can see that in writing his poem, Graves expanded the number of flowers used to create Blodeuwedd from the three mentioned in the *Fourth Branch* to nine, as alluded to in "Cad Goddeu" (if verses from the latter poem does indeed refer to Blodeuwedd; this is likely, given the context of the poem in its entirety, but she is never directly named). Save for two taken directly from "Cad Goddeu", there is no indication of where Graves sourced these additional flowers, so we cannot say that these are traditional to Blodeuwedd's tale. Graves' additions are: primrose, nettle (both mentioned in "Cad Goddeu"), cockle, bean, chestnut, and hawthorn.

It is interesting to note that while these flowers may not be canonical, they certainly support a similar energy to those named in the Fourth Branch and "Cad Goddeu" in several ways, and it is worth looking at the qualities of a few of these additions in order to get a sense of why Graves may have chosen the flowers that he did to include in "Hanes Blodeuwedd". All of Graves' flowers are either white like meadowsweet, or yellow like broom and oak blossoms; perhaps this alludes to Blodeuwedd's appearance, as pale white skin and blonde hair is a common beauty standard in Celtic literature.

Hawthorn (*uath*), like the oak (*duir*), is one of the trees in the ogham tree alphabet. It is a boundary tree often used in hedgerows or grown over holy wells, and through it, the Otherworld can be accessed. This may account in part for its association with Calan Mai (Beltane), that doorway between the Dark and Light Halves of the year. Hawthorn is also known as the May Tree or May Bush, referring to the use of its white blossoms in May Day folkloric practices (when one goes "a-maying", one is ostensibly gathering hawthorn blossoms with which to decorate the outside of the home, but this "gathering of flowers" may have had some sexual connotations as well). In some areas of Britain, folk celebrations of May Day include the selection of a young, unmarried woman as May Queen and crowning her with a wreath of flowers; it is not hard to see a reflection of Blodeuwedd in this practice, but no direct connection can be made, other than that both are representatives of the fertile energies of Spring. Similarly, primrose, a yellow flower that often grows in hedgerows, also has associations with May Day, and like other boundary herbs, it is said to grant fairy Sight. It has protective properties, especially when placed over a threshold, and the blooms themselves are said to be keys that open the door to the Otherworld.

An energetic that appears to be missing from the flowers in the Fourth Branch, but is present in "Cad Goddeu" and Graves, is that of a dangerous beauty. Blodeuwedd's dual nature as dutiful wife and betraying lover, as Flower Face and Owl, is represented by the inclusion of hawthorn and nettle in the herbal formula that creates her. As alluded to by its name, the hawthorn tree sports sharp, spiny thorns as protection, while the nettle plant which grows so wild and abundantly in Britain is also called "stinging nettle" due to the painful reaction caused by the venom on its hair-like spines when it comes into contact with skin. Both plants have powerful healing qualities, and yet both can cause injury as well—an apt representation of the darker side of Blodeuwedd, and perhaps the motivation for including these flowers in alternative, and more modern, accounts of her creation.

For those dedicated to Blodeuwedd, or who want to form a relationship with her, the gathering together of her flowers to create an incense that you can burn, or an energetic elixir that you can take is a meaningful act of devotion. The majority of these flowers require that you harvest them for yourself as most are not sold commercially. The fact that it may take years to assemble all of the components is a reflection of that devotion, and will make the floral mixture, once complete, a worthy offering to this Goddess.

As you obtain them, spend some time working with each of the flowers in turn. Meditate upon each one, seeking out their connections to Blodeuwedd. Consider doing some in-depth research into their medicinal, folkloric, and energetic qualities. When you feel ready to make the mixes, begin with making a blend with the three flowers mentioned in the *Fourth Branch*, the "canonical" blooms, and then start looking for all nine flowers if you feel so drawn. Once you have all of them, compare the three flower blend to the one with nine flowers to feel out the differences—and similarities—between the two blends. Then, going forward, use the one with which you resonate the most as you work with this beautiful and complex divinity.

SOURCES

Allen, David E., Hatfield, Gabrielle. *Medicinal Plants in Folk Tradition: An Ethnobotany of Britain and Ireland.* (Cambridge UK, Portland, Oregon: Timber Press, 2004).

Davies, Sioned, *The Mabinogion* (New York: Oxford University Press, 2007).

Graves, Robert. *The White Goddess: A Historical Grammar of Poetic Myth* (London: Faber & Faber, 1948).

Grieve, Margaret. *A Modern Herbal: The Medicinal, Culinary, Cosmetic and Economic Properties, Cultivation and Folk-Lore of Herbs, Grasses, Fungi, Shrubs & Trees with Their Modern Scientific Uses, Vols.1 and 2.* (Mineola, New York: Dover Publications, 1971).

Hoffman, David. *Welsh Herbal Medicine.* (Aberteifi, Ceregigion:Abercastle Publications, 1978).

Skene, William Forbes. *The Four Ancient Books of Wales.* (Edinburgh: Edmonston and Douglas, 1868).

Nine Flowers: (1) Meadowsweet (2) Broom (3) Cockle (4) Chestnut (5) Nettle (6) Oak (7) Bean (8) Hawthorn (9) Primrose

102

BLODEUWEDD

by Laura Bell

Evening Prayer to Blodeuwedd

BY JULIE BOND

O Blodeuwedd,
Maid of flowers, the Oak, the Broom, and the Meadowsweet;
Lady called forth by Math and Gwydion,
I greet you this Eve.
In the evening the Broom flowers pour forth their scent;
Their sweet fragrance fills the Spring air.
O Maid of flowers turned into an owl,
Bring sweetness to me as I seek to grow wise.
O Blodeuwedd, Flower-Face,
O Lady who made your own choice;
As blossoms garland the land and all Nature blooms forth,
I honour you this Eve and this Spring.

Blodeuwedd (Maiden Queen)

Tammi Boudreau

Words and Music by Tammi Boudreau © 2003. All rights reserved.

Nine Flowers of Blodeuwedd

A Blessing Oil or Perfume Recipe

BY HEATHER KAMINSKI

5/8 dram Jojoba oil (1/8 fluid oz.)
2 drops Lavender
2 drops Melissa
1 drop Sweet Orange
1 drop Palmarosa
1 drop Ylang
1 drop Ho Wood
1 drop Jasmine Absolute
1 drop Rose Absolute
1 drop Vetiver

Because the Nine Flowers of our Goddess don't come in an essential oil form, I chose nine oils which I felt would intuitively blend together to represent the energy of our beautiful Lady Blodeuwedd and Her story.

- Lavender (*Lavendula augustifolia*): Calming, soothing, nurturing and balancing
- Melissa (*Melissa officinalis*): Opens the mind, comforts during times of grief, calms emotions
- Sweet Orange (*Citrus sinensis*): Combats pessimism, unblocks and circulates stagnant energy
- Palmarosa (*Cymbopogon martini* var. *motia*): Reduces anxiety and supports a sense of adaptability
- Ylang Ylang (*Cananga odorata*): Helps one to experience joy and pleasure, promotes sensual awakening
- Ho Wood (*Cinnamomun camphor act linalool*): Helps prepare for spiritual healing
- Jasmine Absolute (*Jasminum gradiflorum*): Release of inhibitions, relieves depression due to emotional repression, diminishes fear, supports comfort within oneself
- Rose Absolute (*Rosaceae*): soothes and heals the heart,

brings a feeling of love, heals despair

- Vetiver (*Vetiveria zizanioides*): Connects with the earth, grounds and protects, sedates and restores, connects one with oneself

Uses

(This is a very strong blend with a high dilution percentage. Use only a small amount at one time and dilute with a carrier oil if necessary.)

- As a blessing oil as per your usual ritual process
- On each chakra point to open and assist in moving blocked energy
- As a perfume on the pulse points to bring the energies of Blodeuwedd with you through your day

Getting It Done Her Way:

The Buffy-Blodeuwedd Connection

BY KATE BRUNNER

" You guys, you're just men—just the men who did this… to her. Whoever that girl was before she was the first Slayer. You violated that girl… made her kill for you because you're weak… you're pathetic and you obviously have nothing to show me! "

-Buffy Summers in "Get It Done"

A woman made of flowers and fluff forsakes her marriage vows, manipulates another man into committing premeditated murder and then runs from the scene of her crimes and her sentence. Admittedly, my initial exposure to Blodeuwedd left me more than a little befuddled. While I was confident there had to be something for me to take away from Her mythology, I realized it was going to take far more work to get at it, to help what I needed emerge from the story, than it had earlier this Cycle.

Blodeuwedd and I *needed* to establish a relationship, a dialogue of some kind. I could see that clearly enough. She was going to be beyond necessary for my Cycle work to continue. But still I was frustrated. During a camping trip I made just before Gwyl Mair, I found myself on the banks of Lake Raven, scrying owls in the embers of our fire. Lady Blodeuwedd seemed impatient to reach me and Her avian messengers appeared with increasing frequency over the next few weeks. I found owls at the craft store, saw them watching me in swirls of paint on the ceiling of a dance studio and found one made of flowers, trees and crescent moons on a clearance priced t-shirt. For my part, I began collecting bits and pieces here and there, looking for a connection, an accessible avenue of approach for us to meet. I collected a

108

handful of oak catkins on a hike with my children, sniffed the wild evening primroses beginning to emerge in clumps all over Texas, ordered some dried meadowsweet and stumbled across a scrollwork pendant that looked Celtic, flowery and owl-like to me all at once. I read and re-read various translations, re-tellings, and poems of Her, listened to songs, sat with the idea of Her in quiet hours, and looked for scholastic commentary, old and new. I could see different perspectives on Her story and sense Her on the periphery. But still I lacked the channel that would open me to Her in the way I was longing for, in the way my work this Cycle called for to continue.

Then in a very mythological quest type fashion, as I began to be quite concerned that Blodeuwedd and I might not establish a solid relationship this Cycle, I came across the words that became the beginning of the key. In an online essay on Blodeuwedd by Anna Franklin, she suggests that one way some people might interpret Her story is as the story of "a woman rebelling against a role decided for her by the men who created her." While she goes on to discuss more thoroughly an interpretation based on ancient themes of seasonal cycles of initiation, Franklin's off the cuff words rang in my head, bouncing from inner wall to inner wall, echoing until they collided with the image of another young woman's mythology stored in my mind. Sitting there at my desk, I think I actually physically shook my head a few times to see if the images would dislodge or if there was solidity to them. They stood their mental and metaphorical ground despite the attempt at cranial seismic activity. And the channel between Blodeuwedd and me began to slide open.

Originally created by Joss Whedon as a movie, the mythology of *Buffy the Vampire Slayer* came into being through Kristy Swanson's performance in a feature length film in 1992. For all the campiness and cult appeal of the original movie, Buffy did not really breathe herself into being for me until the premiere of the WB television series and Sarah Michelle Gellar's portrayal of her beginning in 1997. My freshman year of college, I was instantly drawn to her. Almost twenty years later, I can still connect that one television show to my life in various ways on a regular basis. I will also freely confess to owning the entire series on DVD and to usually watching the whole thing from beginning to end in a rather ritual fashion about once a year. As the mythology of the Slayer unfolded over seven seasons, a prevalent theme existed throughout the show. Buffy was a Slayer unlike any other, redefining the archetype and regularly bucking her own mythological history. She did things her way. She let her instincts guide her. She got confused, got hurt, made mistakes, dealt with them, grew stronger, brought lessons of the past forward and continuously evolved. The more I thought about Buffy through an Avalonian lens, the more I could see the entirety of the series as Buffy's own quest for Sovereignty.

The Buffy-Blodeuwedd connection forged by the initial happenstance of reading Anna Franklin's article was further tempered for me by sitting down to re-watch the fifteenth episode of the seventh and final season, an episode entitled "Get It Done." The episode begins with a prophetic dream in which the First Slayer tells Buffy, *"It's not enough."* Spurred on by this urging and the looming threat of an extremely formidable foe, Buffy undertakes a shamanic journey of sorts to return to the original source of the Slayer's mythic power and see what she can bring back with her to help her fight the largest battle she'd ever faced. There she meets the Shadow Men: elders, magicians, leaders of an ancient patriarchal culture. She learns that the Shadow Men created the Slayer by placing the spirit of a demon inside a captive young girl. The first Slayer was therefore created by men to serve their purpose, to fill the role they chose for her without her input or consent. Pause to marvel at the parallels. In their infinite wisdom, the Shadow Men attempt to repeat the process with Buffy—including the "without consent" part—in order to instill in her the power she needs to defeat her epic opponent. Not surprisingly, Buffy refuses, fighting against them for her freedom.

Craving more to work with, I continued to explore the connection between Blodeuwedd's and Buffy's quests for Sovereignty and the potential breaths of Emergence energy flowing between them on their oddly parallel paths. Published in the fantastic meeting of pop culture and philosophy that is *Buffy the Vampire Slayer and Philosophy: Fear and Trembling in Sunnydale*, Jessica Prata Miller's essay "'The I in Team': Buffy and Feminist Ethics" discusses the emergence of Buffy's sovereignty. In a portion of the essay addressing moral autonomy, Miller (2003) highlights feminist ethicists' historic concerns that "heterosexual women tend to overidentify with the moral perspective and world view of their male partners, preventing... true moral autonomy" (p. 45-6) and uses Buffy as an example of the possibility of achieving feminine moral autonomy while simultaneously stepping outside traditionally masculine paradigms. As she matures, she rejects first the traditional framework of the institutions of the Slayer such as the Watchers and their Council to function independently in the world around her. Eventually, by descending to confront the Shadow Men, she exerts her sovereignty in the face of the very foundation of the Slayer's creation and emerges with her moral autonomy complete. And completely feminine.

Feeling I now had a solid initial grasp on Buffy's transformation, I turned to Jennifer Heath's *On the edge of dream: The women of Celtic myth and legend*, for a deeper look at Blodeuwedd's journey towards feminine moral autonomy. In her creative re-telling of Blodeuwedd's tale, Heath (1998) is rather clear about her interpretation of the goal of Blodeuwedd's own Shadow

Men: Gwydyon, Math and Llew. They intended to create a woman who was "compliant, submissive and manageable" (p. 72). However, she grows into her feminine strength and gradually begins to reclaim her sovereignty, decision after increasingly autonomous decision until they realize she has "emerged far enough from the shadows to rebel against [their] authority" (p. 84).

The rich tapestry woven through me with the warp of Blodeuwedd's chronicle and the weft of Buffy's saga has created quite the energy with which to cloak myself as I engage my own Emergence this year. The twin tales of inspiration have blown away all discernable obstacles to establishing just the healing dialogue Blodeuwedd and I need for Her to work in me as I work on me. In addition to meditative, experiential reflection or ritual and formal scholastic inquiry, I have now also learned to widen the lens somewhat. To include looking at slightly less academic, per say, sources that equally encourage connection between the ancient Avalon and Her evolving modern existence. In other words, I'm getting it done. My way.

REFERENCES

Franklin, A. *BLODEUWEDD*. Last retrieved on March 28, 2011 from http://www.merciangathering.com/blodeuwedd.htm

Grosso, A. (2009). I am free [Recorded by Sisters at the Level 2 Intensive]. On SisterSpace Chant Library [mp3]. Ohio.
Heath, J., *On the Edge of Dream: The women of Celtic myth and legend* (New York, NY: Penguin Putnam Inc), 1998.

Miller, J. P.. "The I in team: Buffy and feminist ethics." In South, J. B. (Ed.), *Buffy the Vampire Slayer and Philosophy: Fear and Trembling in Sunnydale* (Peru, IL: Carus Publishing Company), 2003. (35-48).

Petrie, D. (Writer & Director). (2003). Get It Done [Television series episode]. In J. Whedon (Producer), *Buffy the Vampire Slayer*, Los Angeles, CA.

Blu and Llew

BY SARAH E. ELSBERND

*T*here was once a young boy named Llew who felt very lonely. One day he told two clumsy wizards, Math and Gwydion that he had been feeling sad and wanted a friend, someone his own age. Llew's mother, Arianrhod looked surprised by Llew's request.

"What is a friend?", Math asked.

Gwydion shrugged his shoulders and said, "Someone whom everyone likes?"

Math scratched his head and said, "She should be pretty. That's really important."

Arianrhod wisely shook her head. "It doesn't sound like you know what a friend is. A friend is not simply someone that people like or looks pretty. A friend is someone you respect and can share things with. All three of you have a lot to learn about friendship."

Math and Gwydion thought about it for awhile and decided to create a maiden out of flowers to be Llew's friend, despite what Arianrhod had said. They agreed that Gwydion's friend should be pretty and so they gathered nine different beautiful flowers together. They did not notice that each and every flower they chose had sharp thorns. They were sure that beauty was more important than anything else and so they did not pay attention to the thorns. They waved their wands over the flowers and said some magical words. The flowers formed into a divine young maiden named Blodeuwedd. They decided to call her "Blu" for short. She wore a silver necklace with a yellow stone around her throat and she wore a dress covered with yellow and white flowers.

Llew felt pleased and excited to finally have a friend all his own. Llew happily took her hand and led her to some woods behind his house. He said, "I've always been too afraid to enter these woods. Now that you are here, we will explore! Let's go."

Blu dug her heels into the earth and tugged her hand back. Llew would not let go. She said, "I was created to be your friend. Friends talk. I'd like to sit and talk first before we go anywhere."

Llew scoffed at her words and took a firmer hold of her hand. He dragged her into the woods as he said, "I've waited a long time to go into these woods and we are going whether you want to or not!"

Blu decided to keep quiet and not object to Llew's rudeness. Her yellow stone seemed to grow colder at her throat. She looked around in interest as they walked deeper and deeper into the woods. She saw that the path through the woods forked ahead. One path led into a dark patch of trees and did not look safe. The other path looked safer and less scary. Llew started dragging Blu towards the dark scary path. She dug her heels into the earth again and said, "I do not want to walk down that scary path. Please, let's take this other path, it looks so much nicer!"

Llew stopped walking and looked at her face. He could see that she felt scared. He laughed at her and called her a scaredy-cat, forgetting that he had been afraid to go into the woods by himself. He let go of her hand, stood behind her and pushed her towards the scary path. "We are going this way, I don't care what you say", Llew shouted. Blu knew that the path he was pushing her down was not where she wanted to go. She knew, deep down inside that this path was unsafe. She wanted him to like her so she let him push her where he wanted to go. Her yellow stone felt even colder now.

Blu looked around as they walked deeper into the dark woods. She tried to talk to Llew and become friends with him. She asked him what his favorite colors were and she asked him questions about his mother, Arianrhod. Llew refused to answer her questions and ignored her as they walked. After a while Blu heard some loud rustling in the trees ahead. She peered through the dark woods but could not see anything. She walked faster until she saw a large and fierce snake caught in a hunter's net in a tree. "Please, let's go help that snake, Llew," Blu said.

Llew shook his head and said, "No, that ugly old snake looks mean, we are not going anywhere near her."

Blu became angry. "You have ignored me three times now! Enough! I have been polite and I have tried to be your friend but you keep ignoring what I say and what I want. I will not be ignored any longer," she declared and pulled her hand away from Llew. Her yellow stone began to shine with golden light and grew warm at her throat. She ran over to the snake and freed her from the net. The snake slithered up to a branch in the tree and looked down at Blu and Llew.

Llew stalked over to Blu and shoved her. He glared as he yelled, "You were made to be my friend. You have to be my friend."

Blu calmly replied, "You do not know how to be someone's friend. You don't listen when I talk. You have dragged me and pushed me where you wanted to go. I may have been created to be your friend but I am an individual and can choose for myself. I choose to not go another step with you until you treat me with respect. In order to have a friend you must be a friend."

Llew threw himself on the ground. He screamed in anger and beat the ground with his fists and feet. The snake watched for a bit and then slithered down to the ground next to Blu. "Who is this boy that doesn't know how to be a friend?"

Blu looked into the snake's sparkling black eyes and said, "His name is Llew, Ms. Snake."

"Stand up, Llew," said Ms. Snake in a firm tone.

Llew stood up and glared at Ms. Snake. "She has to be my friend no matter how I treat her," he angrily declared. "Gwydion and Math made her for ME! I don't have to learn how to be a good friend just because she says so!"

Llew and Blu did not realize that Ms. Snake was really Arianrhod in disguise. "Because you refuse to learn how to be a good friend I am going to turn you into an eagle. Once you have learned how to be a good friend you will turn back into a little boy," and Ms. Snake threw off her disguise and stood before Blu and Llew. She waved her hand over Llew and he turned into an eagle and flew away.

Arianrhod turned to Blu and said, "You have learned to speak your truth and stand up for what you believe in. Sometimes people who call themselves your friend will take you down paths that you don't want to go. It is important that you tell these people 'no'. A true friend will want what is best for you. I am impressed by your courage and your strength. By learning how to speak your truth and do what's best you have shown that you know how to be a true friend.

You will have lots of friends who respect you and love you the way you are; for what you believe not the way you look. Math and Gwydion ignored the thorns and only looked at the pretty flowers. If they had noticed the thorns they would have realized that one day you would find your inner strength and become more than just a pretty face."

Arianrhod waved her hand over Blu. "I grant you the ability to become a hunter of the night. When you wish it you will become a beautiful snowy-white owl. You will be a friend of both animals and humans."

Blu slowly began to smile with joy and wonder. She turned herself into a snowy-white owl and flew off in search of friends.

© 2005

... Feathers Soon.

by Alicia Grosso

THE WHITE SPRING

by Kate Brunner

Book Review:

The Owl Service by Alan Garner, Odyssey Classics edition, 2006

BY TIFFANY LAZIC

Sometimes I adore the internet. Those times when you're doing Google searches, putting in odd keywords like "Blodeuwedd" and "owl" and the hit returns a classic British children's book that you would never have stumbled upon otherwise. This is how "The Owl Service" appeared on my computer and, after reading the minuscule blurb, I ordered it, not knowing what to expect. I was an avid reader as a child. Even an avid reader of British authors. Enid Blyton and Rosemary Manning were particularly beloved. But who was this Alan Garner, who was apparently so prolific and admired that he was awarded the Order of the British Empire for Literature in 2001? Some searching seems to have answered that question. The Owl Service was first published in 1967. Publication rights were renewed in 2000. There seem to be a number of years in there (precisely around the time of my British book buying stint) when this title was a bit hard to find.

When the book finally did arrive and I saw the cover, I couldn't wait to dive in. It promised to present the story of Blodeuwedd with a different reflection. I was eager to find other little insights into Her myth through this novel, aimed at children ages 12 and up. Well, I definitely fall into the "and up" category. I was further intrigued by the caption at the bottom of the cover: "Winner of the Carnegie Medal and the Guardian Award". Presumably these are prestigious British literary awards and it is quite a feat for one book to be awarded both. The author biography at the back of the book states that, in 1968, when Alan Garner won these awards, he was the first author to win both for a single book. Anticipation unbridled...

Picture an ancient home in a quiet valley somewhere in Wales. There is a town nearby where all the townsfolk know each other and Welsh is spoken (particularly when you don't want the vacationing English children to understand what you are saying). The homestead has been bequeathed to a young girl, Alison, by her deceased father. She is visiting with her mother, her step-father, Clive and her step-brother, Roger.

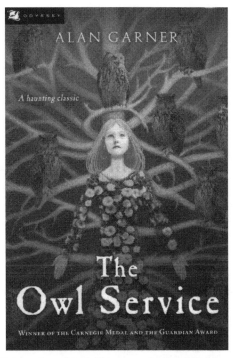

It is summer and the scent of meadowsweet rests in the air. This 'somewhere-in-Wales' is fairly quickly localized when young Roger is informed that the strange slab of rock that he is lolling beside at the river is actually the "Stone of Gronw". Given that this follows on the heels of the discovery of a set of dinnerware with strange flowery designs on it which Alison sees as stylized owls, the pulse of any lover of Welsh mythology quickens.

Balancing the 'fish-out-of-water' folks is a trinity of Welsh characters who weave and deepen the mystery. Most significant is young Gwyn, son of the manor's housekeeper, Nancy. He is befriended by Alison and Roger, being of similar age. As Alison's fascination with owls turns to health-risking obsession, he tries to get to the root of the mystery afoot that his mother and the townsfolk seem to know and seem to be trying to keep from the children. His only ally is the odd, perhaps mad grounds caretaker, Huw, nicknamed "Huw the Halfbacon" Why the catchy moniker? Huw admits to Gwyn at one point that many, many years before he traded horses and greyhounds for some pigs. Curiosity peaked...

This story is a magical and delightful reworking of the Blodeuwedd myth that can be read on many different levels.

On the main level, there is the mystery of a town that becomes the victim of othernatural forces generation after generation. The flavour of living in a small Welsh town depicted is definitely sweet to the taste. Who can't smile while reading when the gossiping townsfolk get in a flap because "Gareth Pugh's black sow ran wild on the mountain and they can't bring her down"? There is meaning in those words. And the townspeople know it.

On a more subtle level, there is the class element which seems to oft be present in British literature. Alison and Roger are very much the young lady and lord of the manor whereas Gwyn is the local help. Differences in how parents treat them, how money is distributed, even how they approach the growing mystery is evident in their sense of place with each other. Gwyn, studying at school in Aberystwyth, has dreams of 'bettering himself' which he shares in confidence with Alison. The stakes in what is unfolding around them are very high for young Gwyn, holding his future in the balance.

And on a sadly poignant level, there are the subtle references to the conflict between the English and the Welsh from a cultural perspective. One of the most touching lines in the book is when Gwyn snaps at Alison, "Don't knock our national heritage, girlie. Them old tales is all we got." This is somewhat touched on in the class differences, but goes deeper to reflect who is caught by the mysterious forces occurring and who is trying to reveal the mystery. Who is trying to control them and who is trying to work with them. Welsh Nancy appears angry and overwrought. Welsh Huw is presented as an old fool. The townspeople are 'rude' in speaking Welsh, in Roger's eyes. But when the veils of a hidden past are lifted, it is their responses that actually made sense.

These different levels give such depth and insight from a slim and quickly read children's novel, giving much fodder for contemplation. Yet, for me, the most delightful moments occur in the slow revelations of Blodeuwedd. After a part of a wall in the billiard room falls, the painting of a woman is revealed. A woman who "was tall. Her long hair fell to her waist, framing in gold her pale and lovely face. Her eyes were blue. She wore a loose gown of white cambric, embroidered with living green stems of broom and meadowsweet, and a wreath of green oak leaves in her hair." And I practically cheered when Huw defends her by saying "She was made for her lord. Nobody is asking her if she wants him".

A treasure in my little collection of Welsh books, I love this tale, "a haunting classic." It is one of those children's books that makes one wonder how that age designation was applied in the first place. As an adult reading it, I was left with much to consider. It felt like a testament and apology to Blodeuwedd for 'doing Her wrong' in the first place and somehow, in those pages, it felt like an answer to an ancient tragic turn of events.

Blodeuwedd

Copyright © 1995/Lori (Llyn) Schneider (BMI)
All Rights Reserved.
www.lori-llyn.com

From Petals to Wings

BY ROBIN CORAK

Prologue

*A*s I sit here composing this letter to you, my dearest child, my heart swells with love and pride. I see so much of myself in you, and yet, you are your own, unique individual and I revel each and every day in watching you grow from a child into a woman. Inquisitive as always, you have often asked me questions that troubled me. Questions about my family, my past, your father. These questions troubled me because the person I was before coming to Glastonbury, before giving birth to you, seems like an incarnation so far removed from my present reality. You couldn't possibly know the shadowed, troubled existence my life had become prior to my rebirth here on the island. I was troubled by your questions because I did not know how— and when—to answer them.

You are poised on the verge of womanhood, my darling, and ready to make your way in the world. You have a right to the answers you seek, whether or not I feel ready to provide them. One of the things I have learned in my training as a priestess is that if we don't face the shadows of our pasts, the demons that plague our existence, we become chained to them, linked forever to the misery they provoke. I have worked hard to free myself from the pain and doubts that pervaded my past, and I do not wish to give them any power over me.

I do not regret what led me to this island, for those events helped shape the woman I am today. Don't misunderstand, I rue the pain that I and those I cared for experienced as a result of our actions, but without those actions I would never have fulfilled my own potential, nor would I have experienced the type of deep love and the joy that only a child can bring. So, I have laid it all out for you in the pages that follow. Please know that I cannot possibly tell my tale objectively, but don't doubt that I tell it with honesty and sincerity.

As you read the pages that follow, I ask of you three things. First, I hope that you will not judge me too harshly nor that these details of my former life will weaken the bond that we have between us. I also implore you to heed the lessons of my life for I believe they will serve you well. Finally, never doubt that you are the greatest gift I have ever received and I feel blessed to have been both your teacher and student as we have travelled this road.

1

"My beautiful Flower Face!"

Whenever my father would use his endearing nickname for me, I would flush all over with a warmth and a knowing that I had somehow made him proud and I would rush into his arms. My father was a distant man and subscribed to the philosophy that showing too much affection would somehow spoil his children. However, he seemed to have a soft spot in his heart for his only daughter and from time to time would indulge my desire to earn his acceptance and love by calling me by my nickname. My brothers would tease me mercilessly about my nickname, though always in a good natured manner. Rather than resenting me for gaining my father's affection, they adored me and treated me as though I was some sort of porcelain doll to be admired and protected at all costs. My mother seemed to feel an odd sense of accomplishment whenever she would witness my father showering me with love. It was as if she felt that she had had a hand in creating a daughter beautiful enough to melt my father's icy exterior and therefore had achieved a remarkable accomplishment.

For as long as I can remember, people have commented on my beauty. My mother went to great lengths to ensure that I was always properly presented to my father and to any of our visitors—my alabaster skin gleaming, my dress feminine and perfectly starched, and not one strand of my long, golden curls out of place. My father's nickname referred to his assertion that my features paralleled the beauty of a thousand stunning yet delicate flowers at the height of spring. Although I did not understand what all of the fuss was about, I soon came to view my beauty as a currency of some sort. It would be a long time before I realized that this currency could also be a curse.

My father, Daffid, was a successful banker. Although we lived reasonably well, he always strived for more, particularly greater wealth and a better standing in society. My mother, Genevieve, had come from a very poor family and she did not like to discuss her upbringing much. She had been very beautiful from a young age and was determined not to live the rest of her life in poverty. She therefore used her only asset—her physical appearance—as a way to improve her station in life. She met my father when she was 16, and they married just a few short months later.

When I was a young girl, I loved to roam the countryside near our house whenever I could manage to escape my mother's watchful eye. I longed to build forts amongst the trees and fight imaginary dragons just as my older brothers did each day. Once, when I was 8 (and long past the age for such silly pursuits as my mother would frequently remind me) I snuck out with my brothers as they ran off to enact their most recent battle against the mythical dreaded villains lurking in the woods. We fought with our imaginary swords and raced to find the treasure. My brothers were quite astounded to find that I was not the helpless little girl that they had come to think of me as, and were quite upset when I bested them both in our final game.

With a mud-slicked gown and a giant grin on my face, I bounded through the door to our home with my two sullen brothers behind me.

"Guess what! I wo—", I began, immediately silenced by the stony glare on my mother's usually pleasant face.

My mother took one look at me and commanded me to go to my room and clean myself up.

Later that night, my mother informed me that I was no longer allowed to play outside with my brothers or venture outdoors without being accompanied by one of our trusted servants.

"Why, Mother?" I protested. "I did not hurt my brothers; they were just upset because I beat them at our games. No one got hurt, I swear it!"

Astounded, my mother scolded, "That is irrelevant, Blodeuwedd! You are far too old to be participating in such childish games!"

"But Mother, I am younger than my brothers and you allow them to—"

"Blodeuwedd, dear, you are a girl. You have responsibilities that are quite different than your brothers. If you are ever to be viewed as a proper young lady and to have the life and privileges a young lady of your standing should have, you cannot risk romping through the forest, dirtying your clothes and acting like a wild thing!"

From that day forward, everything changed. While my brothers were outside shrieking with delight, I was learning proper etiquette and being given piano lessons. My one reprieve was my art. I had always had both a colorful imagination and an ability to picture things vividly inside my head. My mother felt that part of the training for being a proper lady included an education in the arts. The first time I was given an easel and paints, it was as though something had come alive inside of me. I painted a picture of my beloved countryside that was so accurate and yet so vibrant that it almost seemed to flourish with a greater intensity than the land the picture was modeled after. My mother viewed my artistic ability as if it were an extension of my physical beauty and encouraged me to develop my talent.

Sometimes my paintings took on a prophetic tone. I would paint an imaginary landscape in great detail only to be confronted with the same landscape in reality just a few days later during a trip to visit a distant relative of my mother's. I tended not to draw attention to these paintings as I feared that they would cause my parents to be alarmed and might even prompt them to discontinue my art lessons. Although much of my art focused on "safe" topics such as still landscapes and graceful ballerinas, I found that as I grew older I became more and more drawn to art that was less one dimensional and which evoked more emotion. Sometimes my paintings portrayed a beautiful, yet melancholy young girl. These paintings allowed an emotional release as I was unable to express any undesirable emotions such as frustration, grief, or anger in the presence of my family and their friends. Upon seeing one of these paintings, my mother gently but clearly reminded me that people typically did not enjoy viewing art of a sad nature and found happy images to be much more appropriate and delightful. From that point forward, I made sure to focus my art on images and ideas that would result in my parents' acceptance and approval. I still enjoyed the process of bringing my imagination to life through art, yet I began to feel resentful of my parents and the expectations they were increasingly placing upon me.

When I turned 13, my parents decided to enroll me in formal education rather than to have me continue with the private tutors that had long been primarily responsible for my education. Although my brothers had been the only children to receive a formal education, I had always excelled in my studies and was able to do a good amount of the schoolwork that they brought home. My parents' decision to enroll me in the young ladies division of my brothers' school was not due to a concern about any deficiencies in the instruction I had been given thus far; rather, both my mother and father felt that a formal education would allow me to interact with the children of some of the wealthiest families in our region as well as make me more attractive in the future as a potential wife for a wealthy, elite young man. I did not form strong friendships with the other girls as my parents would have liked. I tended to be very shy and it seemed as though I did not have much in common with many of my peers. Yet, I found that I loved school. Each day was a new adventure. I would wake filled with a hunger to learn all that I could. In the afternoons, upon returning home from school, I would devote myself to my studies as well as to my art.

The fall of my 15th year, I was enrolled into an astronomy class. I immediately fell in love with the subject and would spend my evenings out on the deck of my room, staring endlessly at the stars and trying diligently to identify the constellations we had learned about in my class. I began tracking the phases of the moon and often could pinpoint impending bad weather based on subtle changes in the sky. Fearful that my parents would feel that my newfound love would distract me from my other pursuits and ultimately from my destiny of finding a proper husband, I kept my excitement about astronomy to myself and worked hard to ensure that my other studies and duties did not suffer. In astronomy class, however, I found it impossible to contain my enthusiasm and I reveled in the approval and extra attention I received from my teacher, Mrs. Athar.

One day, my parents received a call from Mrs. Athar requesting that they meet with her the following afternoon. I was confused; I had not done anything wrong that I was aware of so I did not understand why Mrs. Athar would want to meet with my family. The next afternoon, my family and I met with Mrs. Athar and after exchanging initial pleasantries, Mrs. Athar began to speak.

"As you no doubt know, Blodeuwedd has proven herself to be quite an intelligent young woman and an accomplished scholar. She appears to have a natural aptitude for astronomy and has the highest grade of any student in her class."

My mother grinned and even my usually stoic, reserved father beamed at this news. He patted my hand and replied, "We are quite proud of Blodeuwedd! We have always known her to excel in her academic pursuits and certainly this class is no exception. Thank you, Mrs. Athar, for taking the time to share this great news with us."

My father was getting up to leave when Mrs. Athar said, "If you could wait but just a moment, sir, there is more."

My father, perplexed, settled back down into his chair.

"As I was saying," Mrs. Athar continued, "Blodeuwedd shows an aptitude for and interest in astronomy that I have rarely seen in my 20 years of teaching the subject. There is an intensive astronomy institute being held this summer and I think that it would be perfect for Blodeuwedd. She would have access to the greatest teachers at one of the greatest observatories in our region. Furthermore, at the end of the institute, the top two students will be eligible for substantial scholarships to one of seven universities offering top notch studies in astronomy as well as in other subject matters. One of the schools even has an art program as well. I would like to submit Blodeuwedd as a candidate for the summer institute."

My heart leapt at the possibilities this opportunity presented. Not only would I be given a chance to study with some of the finest professors, I would also have the chance to be somewhat independent. I leapt up and ran to Mrs. Athar, shouting "Thank you!" and stopped just short of embracing her once I noticed my father's face. His smile had frozen in place and he held up his hand as if to halt the idea from going any further.

Slowly, he said, "Thank you, Mrs. Athar, for taking such an interest in Blodeuwedd. I agree with you that Blodeuwedd is unusually adept and gifted and the institute sounds wonderful, but Blodeuwedd has other plans for the summer. Unless there is anything else, we will be on our way."

"Wait!" I cried. "I don't have any plans, Father! I so want to do this. Please, I will never ask you for anything again! Please, Father, I..."

My father sternly interrupted me by saying, "Blodeuwedd, I have made my decision and the answer is no."

"Sir, perhaps I was not clear. This is an amazing opportunity, the likes of which Blodeuwedd may never again encounter in her life. This could open up so many doors for her! I assure you that there is plenty of supervision so it's not as though she will be left unattended. If it's a question of money, I..."

"Enough!" my father yelled. His unexpected outburst left us all frozen in place. "Mrs. Athar, I assure you that this has nothing to do with money. I provide quite well for my family and am in need of no one's charity. Should we so desire, we would have no difficulty in paying for Blodeuwedd's tuition to the summer institute or to one of the universities you mentioned for that matter. It just so happens that Blodeuwedd has another destiny waiting for her and her attention must be focused on that. Thank you, again, for the opportunity but we must decline. Good day, Mrs. Athar."

My father strode from the room without another word. My mother, as if awakened from a daze, slowly picked up her coat, and smiling feebly at Mrs. Athar, gently grabbed my arm and began to lead me out of the room. I could not bring myself to look at Mrs. Athar and instead mutely followed my mother with my eyes cast downward, my body racked by quiet yet powerful sobs. I spent the rest of the evening locked away in my room, refusing to come downstairs. For years, I had begun feeling more and more resentful of the opportunities that were withheld from me because of my gender and the expectations that were imposed upon me because of my parents' aspirations and the value they saw in my physical beauty. I had continued to repress these feelings, never allowing them the chance to surface or make themselves known in anyone's presence but my own. Having been given a glimpse of a future that excited me only to have the vision destroyed in an instant seemed to ignite all of the feelings of anger and frustration I had repressed, resulting in an outburst beyond anything my mother had ever seen.

"It's not fair!" I screamed. "Shouldn't I be rewarded for all of my hard work rather than punished? Shouldn't I be allowed to make at least some decisions regarding my life? I have done everything—EVERYTHING—you have asked me to do. Why? Why couldn't you let me do this one thing? It's not fair!"

I collapsed into sobs as my mother held me and caressed my hair. "Shh…" she murmured. "I know. I know it's not fair. Life isn't fair sometimes. You have to understand, Blodeuwedd, your father is not trying to punish you. He is trying to ensure that you will have security, a good future with a good man. We know that you have worked hard in school and have done what we have asked. Don't you see? We want so much more for you. We want you to have the world at your fingertips. Most men want an intelligent woman, to be certain. They want to know that the mother of their children will possess some level of intelligence and education so that this may be passed on to their children. Yet a woman who is too intelligent, too ambitious—well, this type of woman, no matter how beautiful, does less to attract a man and more to repel him. Men are threatened by women of this stature."

I stared at her, dumbfounded and wild eyed. "Why, Mother? All of my life, you have drilled into me how important it is to attract a man. You have trained me and trained me on how to be a proper young lady and a proper wife. Why is it so important to you? Have you ever considered that maybe I don't want to be a proper wife? Would it displease you and father so much for me to be a successful, happy, independent woman? Why, Mother? Is it because you never had that opportunity? Is it possible that you are jealous that I might have the opportunities you never had?"

Crying, my mother slapped me across the face and I shrank back in surprise, rubbing my cheek. Startled at her own reaction, my mother quickly composed herself and began to speak.

"Blodeuwedd, you must never say such things. I only want what's best for you. So let's say you went to this institute and perhaps even on to university. What then? Even if you were to have a career of some sort, that won't be enough forever. Eventually, you will want a man to settle down with, children even. What's more, you will need a man—few women earn enough to support themselves in the manner to which you have been accustomed. You are a beautiful young woman, Blodeuwedd, but beauty fades. If you take too long pursuing your own interests, how will you ever find a proper husband to support you when you are competing with younger women who are also beautiful and who are more suitable for the type of man you desire? You have a father who is successful and who supports this family quite well. You have never known, Blodeuwedd, what it is like to be poor. You have never wondered where your next meal will come from. You have come from a good family and have been admired for your beauty all of your life and thus you have never known what it feels like to be unwanted. I know what it feels like to have to fight for your survival. I know what it feels like to be unwanted, Blodeuwedd, and I know what it feels like to be alone. I fought hard to escape that and that is why I have also fought so hard to ensure that you will never have to experience that type of pain. If you cannot put your own desires aside to do what's best for you, perhaps you will think about what's best for your father. Do you want this family to be burdened by the choices you make? Do you want your father to be embarrassed by his only daughter?"

Oh, the war that raged within me! The very thought of fulfilling the destiny that my parents had laid out for me left me feeling suffocated. The only thing more powerful than that feeling of dread was the pain I would feel imagining the disappointment on my father's face should I choose to betray him and my mother. I had been bred to view my main purpose in life as pleasing others. This, along with my beauty, were the few if not the only traits that had ever earned me the acceptance and love that I so longed for and needed. I could not risk losing my parents' approval and love. I could not risk having my father never look at me with pride, never call me his "Flower Face" again. From that day forward, I learned to suppress my desires and align all of my choices with the image my parents had so carefully cultivated for me.

"Blodeuwedd! Blodeuwedd! Come quickly!"

My mother's excited summoning of me caused me to panic. I ran down the stairs as fast as I could, my cheeks flushing bright red at the effort.

"What is it, Mother? What's wrong?"

"Nothing's wrong, dear. Your father has just called to let me know that we will be having a guest for dinner—a Mr. Mathowny. He's apparently very wealthy and your father is hoping to be able to convince him to open an account with your father's bank. He has a son, Lew, who will be joining us. From what your father told me, Lew is quite handsome and wealthy in his own right in addition to being heir to one of the largest fortunes in history."

This explained her excitement, I thought. Ever since I had turned 18, my life had been filled with social event after social event in an attempt on my parents' part to introduce me to society and to find me a proper husband. I had grown weary of my mother's incessant speculation about the various eligible bachelors circulating amongst high society. It seemed as though my father had at least one of these bachelors over for dinner or some social gathering each week in an attempt to introduce them to his lovely, smart, well-bred daughter. To be honest, I could care less about marriage—a feeling that was only compounded by the fact that most of these men were either too old, too boring, or just plain too insufferable for me to imagine living happily ever after with them. I was relieved when, for one reason or another, my parents' attempts to marry me off did not work out. Still, I kept up appearances and played the part of the gracious hostess, never letting on that I was desperate for the evening to be over. I was sure that tonight's dinner with Lew and his father would not be any different.

I waited patiently as my mother and our housemaid drew my bath, selected just the right dress, and helped me to get ready for the evening. My mother must have been quite impressed with my father's description of the gentlemen joining us for dinner, for she seemed to put extra thought and effort into helping me get ready so that even I was stunned to finally see my reflection in the mirror. I was wearing a dress of the finest linen which managed to accentuate my curves without being improper. The rose color of the dress seemed to both contrast with my porcelain toned skin and to bring out just the slightest hint of blush in my cheeks. My blue eyes appeared even larger and more luminous than usual, and my long flaxen hair looked like spun gold.

I was used to receiving admiring glances from gentlemen—especially those attending my father's social events. What I was not used to was returning the gesture with an admiring glance of my own. Lew was quite unlike the other men who had come to our house in recent weeks. He was tall and slender, with wavy ebony hair and amber eyes framed by long, dark lashes. He was dressed impeccably and was obviously well mannered as he made sure to pull my chair out for me and compliment me on my dress. I tried to hide my surprise and admiration by focusing on the conversation at hand but Lew was charming and I found myself drawn to him. At the other events my father had hosted in his attempts to introduce me to an eligible bachelor, I felt as though the evening would drag on with each minute lasting a lifetime. With Lew, however, time flew by in an instant and I was both surprised and a bit saddened when Lew and his father rose to thank my parents and depart for the evening.

I could tell by the jubilant manner in which my parents bid me goodnight that they were very pleased by the evening's events and proud of their beautiful young daughter. The next day my father rushed into the house upon arriving home, calling for my mother and I to come downstairs.

"Blodeuwedd, I talked with Mr. Mathowny today and he said that Lew was quite taken with you. He wanted to know if you were available for dinner this evening. I told him that you were. Lew will be here to pick you up at 7 pm sharp. I have a very good feeling about this, Flower Face! I picked you up a little something on my way home as a good luck charm for this evening. The sales girl assured me that it was the perfect complement for someone with eyes the color of a stormy sky."

My father held out a square box wrapped with a blue satin bow. I took the box, unsure of what it could hold. My breath caught in my throat as I opened the lid and found a necklace and earrings with sapphires of the deepest blue I had ever seen offset by diamonds which sparkled and shone, creating their own light.

"Father, these must have cost a fortune! Surely you cannot…"

My father cut me off, smiling, and said, "Blodeuwedd, dear, haven't your mother and I taught you that when a respectable man offers you a gift such as this, the only appropriate response is a simple thank you? Now, run along and get ready or you will be late, and no man likes to be kept waiting."

I laughed, kissed my father on the cheek, and ran upstairs with my mother in tow to select just the right outfit to wear with my father's gift.

For the next several weeks, Lew courted me incessantly with romantic dinners, walks in the park, and endless trinkets, flowers, and gifts. I felt myself falling for him despite my desire to remain a young girl unburdened by the responsibilities of being the "proper wife" that my mother and father longed for me to be. It was as if Lew knew all of my secret romantic desires for he always knew just the right thing to say or do. My parents quickly came to treat Lew as if he were their own son, and he easily endeared himself to my brothers. Finally, after a mere few months of showering me with his affection and attention, Lew asked my father for my hand in marriage. Although I knew that this would eventually happen and did not unwelcome the thought of spending my life with Lew, I felt the briefest flare of resentment at the interaction between Lew and my father. After all, no one had asked me what I thought about getting married. No one had bothered to consult with me at all. Instead, everyone had just assumed that I was elated to finally be fulfilling the destiny set forth for me. After all, hadn't everything in my life led up to this moment?

My mother threw herself into the preparations for our wedding. I immersed myself in this as well, though I felt more like a bystander than an active participant. However, I found that my involvement in the wedding preparations —limited though it might have been—prevented me from addressing the seeds of doubt that were beginning to take hold in my mind. Lew had been less attentive and more reserved ever since our engagement. It wasn't as if he seemed less attracted to my beauty, it was more as though he did not seem to be as engaged in our conversations. I noticed increasingly that Lew would make decisions without regard for my thoughts or opinions and instead just assumed that I would feel as he did.

I knew that Lew's mother and father had separated when he was very young and that he did not have a close relationship with his mother. Yet I was troubled by his immediate and sharp reaction when I asked if his mother would be coming to the wedding. Adamant that she would not be attending, he made it clear that this was not a subject that we would be addressing again. Some part of me dreaded our wedding day, knowing that despite my love for Lew, I would never feel free or fulfilled once we were betrothed. Yet, I pushed these feelings aside and told myself I was being selfish or was just having cold feet. I was determined to make this work and make Lew and my family happy thereby ensuring that I would continue to receive their love and acceptance. Besides, I was not strong enough or brave enough to stand on my own, and really, what other choice did I have?

My wedding day was overwhelming. Everything had been carefully orchestrated, and every detail was executed with military like precision. I felt like a puppet, simply going through the motions, being moved along from place to place, until it was time to say my vows. My hands trembled and I felt as though the world were closing in on me. When the priest asked me if I would take Lew as my husband, it was as if time stopped. Visions of my future rushed into my head. Possibilities of what could be collided with what was and I could feel a part of me begging to let these possibilities live, silently begging to answer from within the deepest part of me what I really wanted rather than giving the answer that I felt compelled to give. Voice trembling and barely audible, I gave in to my fears and cemented my fate with two simple words—"I do".

It was not as though I did not love Lew, for I truly cared deeply for him and in so many ways he strived to make me happy. I yearned for his acceptance no less than I had desired hearing the pride in my father's voice when he said my name. As with my father, I found that much of Lew's contentment with and pride in his new bride had more to do with my physical appearance and my ability to play with near perfection the role of a rich, successful man's wife. Yet the more I gave in to my need for approval from Lew, the less I began to know myself, until I found myself becoming a hollow, paler version of the young woman I once was.

Of course, these realizations did not happen overnight. The first few months following our wedding brought a whirlwind of activity. As a wedding gift, Lew's father had bought Lew and me a large, lavish home not far from his own opulent residence. Despite being trained and molded all of my life for the responsibility of running a household and attending to my husband, I felt far from equipped to fulfill Lew's expectations of me. Fortunately, Mr. Mathowny had agreed to release his longtime employee, Hildy, so that she could come work for us, assisting me in ensuring that household and society obligations were met. Even with Hildy's help I found myself struggling to earn Lew's admiration, but eventually I began to feel more at ease and confident in my new role.

In the early weeks following our marriage, Lew was attentive and forgiving of my flaws and lack of knowledge regarding his preferences. He made sure to spend time with me and indulged me in my habits, my questions, and even my suggestions. However, as time passed, Lew became more involved in his work and soon it was rare that the two of us would have the opportunity to spend any quality time alone together. My increasingly solitary days spent in the immense, spotless abode that was now my home caused me to experience a loneliness which was further fueled by the hours of introspection that I could not avoid as I fulfilled my mind-numbing daily obligations. The irony was that just as I was beginning to experience greater independence due to Lew's absences, my husband began exerting more and more control over the most minute details of my existence, ranging from what I wore to who I talked to. Yet, I continually endeavored to justify my husband's preferences and to work endlessly to solicit his approval.

My sole saving grace during this time was my relationship with Hildy. Hildy had been with the Mathownys for several years and sometimes I thought she knew Lew better than he knew himself. Not only was Hildy tremendously supportive and helpful in my efforts to excel in my new role, I found her to be very caring and nurturing and I came to consider her a friend. I wanted desperately to better know and understand the man I had married, beyond his preferences, mundane opinions, and basic facts of his upbringing. I wanted to know how he became the man he was today, what his dreams were, and the essence of who he was at his very core.

Lew was quite unwilling to share this side of himself with me, just as he was unwilling to look beyond who I was on the surface, the vision of me that he had created in his mind. It did not seem that Lew felt threatened by my attempts to get to know him better, he just didn't seem to see the point. Hildy had been responsible for the management of Mr. Mathowny's household since before Lew was born, and once Lew's mother left, she became ultimately responsible for his day to day care. I often asked her to share her stories of Lew, and I frequently had a difficult time reconciling the adventurous, caring young boy that Hildy described with the increasingly stern, distant man I had married.

One day I took the risk of asking Hildy about Lew's mother. I had been curious about her for some time, but reluctant to broach the subject given Lew's reaction to my previous questions about his mother. I could tell that Hildy was hesitant to share what she knew, but upon seeing the sincere, earnest look upon my face, she began to unravel the tale.

"Lew's father comes from a very wealthy, elite family. Logan Mathowny, Lew's grandfather, had arranged for Lew's father, Phillip, to marry the daughter of a successful businessman who had been heir to a great family fortune. The marriage was intended to establish a strengthened alliance between the two families. Lew's father was all set to marry this young woman…until he met Arianne. Arianne was unlike any woman that Phillip had met. Headstrong as a young child, Arianne had been sent by her parents to live with her aunt in a small community of women in Glastonbury. These women—and the girls who were occasionally sent to live with them—were skilled in the old ways."
"The old ways?" I asked. "What do you mean by that?"

"The old ways?" Hildy replied with a wise, yet impish smile. "Why, they are the ways of our mothers, grandmothers, and their mothers before them. The long forgotten ways of our ancestors—how to heal, plant lore, working in harmony with nature, even prophesying the future. The ways of the priestesses in the legends and stories you were taught as a child. Did you think that everything in those stories was purely imaginary? There is a seed of truth in everything, my dear. Many of those stories were passed on from generation to generation, mother to child, as a way to preserve the knowledge that was becoming increasingly forgotten or forbidden.

Arianne learned these ways and lived with her aunt and the women until she was 18, when she was summoned by her mother and father. Arianne had not intended to stay long with her parents, but as a result of random, synchronicitous events, she met Phillip Mathowny and they fell in love."

"What about the arranged marriage?" I asked.

"Well, Phillip told his father that there was only one woman he wanted to marry now, and that was Arianne. His father, of course, was quite upset and threatened to disinherit him, but Logan Mathowny learned that Arianne was pregnant. Devastated, Logan told Phillip that this would ruin the family's reputation and would not end well. He tried to persuade Phillip to let him talk with Arianne, to send the girl away with more than enough money to ensure that she would be well cared for, but Phillip was defiant and said that there was no way he would allow that to happen. Phillip assured his father that everything would be fine and so Logan reluctantly allowed Phillip to move forward with the intended marriage. However, whereas Phillip had always been the golden child in his family, his father soon began favoring Phillip's younger brother. The breach in the relationship between Phillip and his father never quite healed, despite Phillip's increasingly extraordinary efforts to get back in his father's good graces.

Arianne was not used to the ways of the world outside of her existence in Glastonbury and she was not used to relying on others—such as Phillip—to make her way in the world. Phillip, for his part, was charmed by Arianne's candor, admiring of her strength, and awed by her maturity and independence which was in striking opposition to the young ladies from elite society that he was used to meeting. However, as Phillip's responsibilities grew and he felt increasingly pressured to achieve success, provide for his new family, and maintain his reputation and position within his family and society, he became less enchanted with Arianne's insistence that she be an equal partner in their marriage. Furthermore, Phillip had been spoiled much of his life and was not used to being told "no" by anyone. Shortly after the baby was born, Arianne realized that she and Phillip had very different perspectives on how their child was to be raised.

Arianne firmly believed that Lew should be brought up with much love and affection yet he must also learn accountability and the importance of hard work. Arianne did not want Lew to have everything handed to him on a silver platter, and she wanted him to grow up with a respect for women as his equals rather than his subordinates. Phillip, in contrast, felt that Lew should be raised as he had been—with the world at his fingertips. Phillip loved his son deeply, but much as his relationship with his own father had been, Phillip felt that a relationship between a son and father should be built on respect rather than affection. Phillip adhered to his father's parenting philosophy that overt pride and acceptance of one's son must be contingent upon the child's accomplishments, willingness to fulfill his father's expectations, and an ability to uphold the positive reputation and standing in society which the Mathowny family had cultivated over many, many years. In one of their more heated arguments, Phillip exclaimed to Arianne that continuing to show Lew unconditional affection and love would simply weaken the child and that her insistent desire to instill in Lew a belief that women, too, could be independent, equal to men, and make great contributions to society would ill prepare him for the realities of life."

"I don't understand," I interrupted. "I thought that Arianne's independence was part of what attracted Phillip to her."

"Oh, it was," Hildy continued. "But like most of us the first time we fall in love, Phillip was naïve. He had never been without his father's support and approval, and he was just beginning to realize the challenges brought on by his decision to defy his father and claim his independence. Things had always come easy to Phillip, and now he was having to stand on his own, build his own success and break free from his father's shadow. Phillip had always had a close relationship with his father, and now that he had a son of his own, he greatly missed this relationship as well as the public declarations of pride his father had previously bestowed upon him. Logan Mathowny constantly chided his son in subtle but effective ways and this served to both erode Phillip's confidence in himself and his choices and to harden his heart. Phillip began to resent Arianne. This allowed Logan to plant within Phillip seeds of doubt about their relationship. Arianne saw what was happening and tried to talk with Phillip, but to little avail. She became increasingly troubled about their relationship, and perhaps most importantly, about the implications for her child should he be raised according to Logan Mathowny's beliefs. When Arianne could bear it no further, she informed Phillip that she intended to leave and to take her son with her.

Arianne's departure would cause Phillip some grief, to be sure, but he would learn to bear it. What he could not and would not bear was Arianne's assertion that he would be without his son as well. With great hesitation and humiliation, Phillip turned to his father for help. Logan Mathowny used his wealth and his connections to ensure that Arianne would not make good on her threats. Logan took advantage of Arianne's concern for her son, and was very convincing in his description of the harsh, bitter life that awaited both Arianne and Lew should she choose to raise him as a single mother with no money, no connections, and no one to support her. Arianne was further told that should she choose to leave Lew in his father's care, he would have the best that life had to offer and she was assured that she would be handsomely provided for and would still be granted a role in Lew's life. In case this was not enough to sway her, Logan emphasized that should Arianne persist in her attempts to leave with her child, the Mathowny family's resources would allow them to retrieve Lew by any means necessary, no matter how long it took.

Scared and alone, Arianne felt as though she had few options. Her parents were old and poor and would not be able to accommodate two more mouths to feed. Arianne had not had contact with her aunt in some time and was not even sure where her aunt currently resided. She thought about the idea of taking Lew and travelling back to Glastonbury, but she did not want to risk exposing or endangering the community of women she so loved. Although it caused her great pain, she did as Logan insisted and left Lew with his father. The Mathowny's did keep their promise to provide for Arianne financially, with the caveat that should she attempt to take Lew or impose herself in Lew's life inappropriately, the support would stop. Of course, this caveat greatly restricted her ability to interact with her son, and Phillip went to great lengths to paint an unfavorable portrait of Arianne as a terrible, selfish woman who profited off of her abandonment of her son.

For a time, Arianne travelled by herself back to Glastonbury for much needed solitude and healing. She was reunited with her aunt, and shared with her aunt everything that had happened. Arianne became immersed in the work of the community, and eventually found herself in a leadership role. Although she was both literally and figuratively many miles away, Arianne kept tabs on her son. Arianne was proud of Lew's accomplishments, but disheartened by just how much Lew would follow in the footsteps of his father and grandfather. Phillip had gone to every length to raise Lew in much the manner that he himself had been raised and to ensure that Lew would not make the same mistake he had made as a result of falling in love with Arianne. For this reason,

Phillip invested a great deal of time and energy into forming Lew's ideas about women and marriage and in helping Lew to find an appropriate candidate to be his bride when the time was right.

Arianne felt that Lew's view on women and life in general were quite limited if not distorted and she feared for the young man that Lew was turning out to be, feared that he would never know himself, fulfill his true potential, or find deep, lasting happiness. A small part of her shuddered at the thought of Lew's future bride being exposed to the pain that she had lived through or of Lew perpetuating a dynasty of young men who saw nothing wrong with playing god or young women believing it was their destiny to be ruled by men who saw them as having so little of substance to offer. Arianne returned from Glastonbury to forge a stronger bond with her son and to expose him to other possibilities and views, but by that time it was too late. Phillip held too much influence over Lew and Lew, for his part, had grown to deeply resent and perhaps even fear the image of Arianne that his father had portrayed. Lew, robbed of a mother and ignorant of the truth regarding what really happened all of those years ago when Arianne left, shunned her attempts to regain her rightful place in his life. Unfortunately, dear, because Lew never had a chance to experience as a child the nurturing yet complex relationship one has with a mother, or sister, or any female for that matter, his views on love and the relationship between a husband and wife have been naturally somewhat rigid and…well, incomplete."

"But you were there, Hildy, you cared for him and loved him."

"Ay, that is true," Hildy said, smiling. "But you mustn't forget that although I adored Lew and did my best to care for him, I was, in the end, merely an employee. I came to love Lew over the years as if he were my own, but I never forgot that I worked for the Mathowny's and when Lew grew older and understood my role, he never forgot either."

I sat there, stunned. This was too much to take in and yet, I had to somehow come to grips with all that I had heard for Hildy's story provided the only clues, the only insight I had into my husband. Emotions warred within me—anger over Logan's betrayal of both his son and Arianne, confusion and frustration surrounding Logan's views and Phillip's inability to stand strong, and grief over Lew's loss and Arianne's heartbreak. Despite my frustration with Phillip's choices, I felt grief for him as well, for he had lost his one true love and would never again experience the depth of happiness he had felt when he first fell in love with Arianne. Besides, how could I judge him? Hadn't I, too, been unable to stand up to my father and forge my own path? I felt a rush of compassion towards Lew and a strong desire to somehow protect him and make up for all that he had lost when Arianne left.

The emotion that surprised me the most was my resonation with and curiosity about Arianne. I had never allowed myself the independence and confidence in my own abilities that seemed to have come so easily to Arianne, yet for some strange reason, I found myself drawn to Hildy's description of her as though Arianne were a kindred spirit in some way. I was fascinated with the concept of a woman—no less a community of women—exercising control of their own fate and supporting other women in the process and all without the interference or assistance of men. Then there was their practice of what Hildy had called "the old ways". Although I had never heard the term before, I felt a stirring within me upon hearing those words, as if I could somehow gain the barest glimpse, the tiniest knowing of what these words meant. I chuckled at my foolishness, for how could this possibly be? I began to think that some of what Hildy had told me about Arianne's life was nothing but a tale, a legend of some sort. For how had Hildy known all of this?

"Hildy," I asked, breathless. "How do you know about all of this? How do you know what became of Arianne?"

Fear flashed in Hildy's eyes, and I immediately assured her that I would keep her confidence and not share with another soul what she had told me and was about to tell me.

"Oh, Blodeuwedd, I should not be telling you this. If Lew or his father found out, I could lose my job! I have faith in you, sweet girl, that you will not betray me. Do you remember when I told you that Arianne kept tabs on Lew? She did this through me. I have a great deal of love and admiration for Arianne, and over the years she has become one of my dear, dear friends. I was young and naïve when I began working for Phillip Mathowny, and I could not bear the thought of a mother being separate from her son, not knowing what would become of him. Of course, there wasn't much I could do to repair Lew's image of his mother—or all women for that matter. At least I was able to reassure Arianne that her son was healthy and happy and well cared for. I haven't seen or heard from her in some time, however. I assume that she has returned to the safe haven that exists for her in Glastonbury as she has been wont to do in the past."

"I wish I could have known her, though I doubt I will ever get the chance. You know, I asked Lew about his mother shortly before our wedding", I admitted. "Yes?" Hildy asked, surprised. "What did Lew say?"

"I simply wanted to know if his mother would be at the wedding. I had never met her nor had I heard Lew say much about her and I wanted to know all that I could about my husband to be. I thought perhaps the wedding would give me an opportunity to meet his mother, but Lew became angry and was quite adamant that she would not be attending and that I was not to broach the subject again."

Hildy was quiet for some time and seemed to be grappling with something. Finally, she said, "That is unfortunate, dear, for something tells me that Arianne would have loved to meet you as well."

3

Two years went by, but rarely a day passed when I did not think about Hildy's confession. From time to time, she would share other bits and pieces of Lew's childhood, and I would once again feel a renewed determination to make our marriage work and a fiery desire to provide Lew with the love, affection, and nurturing that he did not receive as a little boy. Lew did not make these attempts any easier, however. He flourished in his job and was quickly becoming known as the most promising young lawyer his field had seen in quite some time. I was reminded constantly by my parents, my brothers, and our friends how lucky I was to have such a charming, handsome, and successful husband. Lew was not quite as charming at home, that is, when he was at home. Our life together became brief interludes of togetherness punctuated by increasingly longer times spent apart. Lew often worked late hours, and his work had recently required him to travel. When we were together, Lew was often distant and very particular about what I wore, how I presented myself, and how the household was to be managed. He was still very complimentary of my beauty and occasionally would reward my attempts to please him with a demonstration of affection, but his efforts seemed hollow. He was unwilling to open up to me and would either laugh or scorn my attempts to engage him in a meaningful conversation.

One day, shortly after Lew left, I was puzzled to hear a knock on our door. Thinking perhaps that he had forgotten something, I opened the door and was astounded when the beautiful, serene older woman standing there held out her hand and said, "It's a pleasure to finally meet you, Blodeuwedd. I am Arianne."

Once I recovered from my initial shock, I led Arianne into the sitting room and called for Hildy. Upon seeing Arianne, Hildy rushed to embrace her, tears streaming down her face. Hildy quickly regained her composure and left to prepare some tea and pastries for us, and for a moment we just sat there in silence, taking each other in. Finally, I spoke.

"How did you know…I mean, does Lew know…", I trailed off, unsure of what to say.

"It's ok," Arianne said, and smiled, putting me at ease. "No, Lew doesn't know that I am here. I waited until I saw him leaving before I approached your house. Unfortunately, I doubt my son would appreciate my efforts to get to know his wife. I intend to leave before he returns. I don't wish to cause any trouble for you, Blodeuwedd, so if you wish for me to leave right now, I will understand."
"No!" The word came out more emphatically than I had intended. "I do not wish for you to leave. It's wonderful to finally meet you. Hildy has told me so much about you."

"I have heard a great deal about you as well. Hildy greatly admires you, and she seems to feel that Lew made a very prudent decision in asking you to be his wife."

The next few hours flew by as Arianne told me more about her life and regaled me with tales of the women in Glastonbury. My head spun with the possibilities her stories presented, yet the reality in her stories seemed so fleeting, so impossible when compared to my existence. I asked Arianne how it was possible to have a society wherein women were free to do as they chose. "Blodeuwedd, the women on this island are priestesses. They do not dislike men, but they do not rely on any man to complete their existence or to tell them what to do. They answer to no one but the goddess. The goddess we worship knows that without cooperation, harmony, equality, and respect for each other's differences, no society, and certainly no individual, can truly thrive. The ways of the society you live in are out of balance. They do not serve you, and they certainly do not serve the men who hold all of the power. It is an illusion. It is not a contradiction for the women of my community to pursue their own interests, their own paths while still working cooperatively to support each other. Yes, there is freedom there—freedom unlike anything you have probably ever experienced. But with freedom, Blodeuwedd, there are also responsibilities. You reap the consequences of what you sow—good or bad. While there is no one there to stand in your way of happiness, there is also no one there to take the responsibility or blame should things go wrong. To be a priestess, one must be willing to accept both the freedom and responsibility sovereignty grants. One must be willing and able to be both vulnerable and strong."

I was considering what Arianne had said, when I heard the door shut and Lew calling out for me. I froze, unsure of what to do. There was no time, no way to get Arianne out of the house unseen. Lew walked into the room, talking while his attention was focused on a piece of paper in his hands. He looked up and saw his mother, and his face grew pale and then slowly, but surely, he began to flush. His voice was icy cold as he began to speak.

"Mother, what a …well I wish I could say it was a nice surprise but we both know I would be lying. What on earth are you doing here?"

"I just happened to be in the neighborhood, and thought I would drop in. Blodeuwedd told me you weren't here and I am afraid I was rather enthusiastic in my desire to get to know Blodeuwedd once I learned that she was your wife." Lew's face contorted with fury and he moved his gaze from his mother to me. For the first time since I had known Lew, I felt scared. Arianne must have picked up on this for she quickly drew Lew's attention back to her.

"Lew, I am so sorry. Truly I didn't mean to impose. Please don't blame Blodeuwedd. She was just acting as the proper hostess and in fact had just suggested that perhaps I should leave and wait to return at a more convenient time for you. I can see that this isn't a good time so I will show myself to the door. Goodbye, my dear."

Without another glance towards me, Arianne walked towards Lew, patted him gently on his arm, and left. Neither of us spoke for a few moments. When the silence became unbearable, I began to stride from the room but Lew stopped me.

"What was she doing here?"

"She told you, Lew, she simply asked if you were home. I didn't realize at first who she was. Honestly, Lew, I didn't mean to…"

"You didn't mean to what?" Lew roared. "You know how I feel about …that woman. She is not to set foot in this house again."

Perhaps I was feeling empowered by my conversation with Arianne, for irritated and feeling a sudden injustice over what had happened, I proclaimed, "Lew, she's your moth—"

My words were cut short by the sound of Lew's hand striking my cheek and the stinging, sharp pain that followed. I was stunned at the realization that he had just slapped me.

Lew looked shocked as well by his actions. He moved toward me, presumably to embrace me, to make sure that I was alright, but I instinctively shrunk back. A look of hurt flashed in his eyes, and he slowly walked past me. Just before leaving the room, he turned back and softly said, "Blodeuwedd, I'm…I don't consider Arianne to be my mother. I think it would be best if you would refrain from speaking with her. You don't know what she's like. She is a selfish, delusional woman, and I don't want her filling your head with all sorts of foolish ideas. I know you are a good woman, Blodeuwedd, and I know that you will honor my wishes." With that, he left the room.

I considered taking a stand right then and there. I contemplated leaving, but where would I go? Who could I turn to? My father's business had increased tenfold since my marriage to Lew, and he enjoyed the status in society that our marriage provided him. My brothers considered Lew to be a great friend, and truly their views on women's roles weren't that much different than Lew's. I should have felt strong, indignant over Lew's treatment of me. I should have believed in my ability, my right to have a life of my own, to have opinions of my own, and to be loved because and not in spite of my individuality. I should have been as strong as Arianne seemed to be. In that moment, however, I felt like a little girl. I was the most vulnerable, most scared I had ever been in my life. The possibilities of a different life thrilled me, but my fear shackled me, tricked me into thinking that I was more bound to Lew now than ever before.

I did not see or hear from Arianne again. This provoked in me both a sense of relief and a feeling of sorrow. Hildy did not speak of the incident, and though our friendship remained strong, we carefully avoided having any further conversations about Lew's past or his mother. Each day the cadence of my life as Lew's wife became more automatic, more deeply ingrained in me. This was both comforting and terrifying, for although going through the motions provided me with a sense of security, I felt suffocated by the knowledge that I was dying inside.

About a month after Arianne's visit, Lew began working on the case that he said would propel his career. He informed me that he would be travelling out of town for a week in order to do some research for the upcoming trial. I tried hard not to show Lew the fear I felt inside at his words. Lew's extended absence would mean that I would have time on my hands to think, to do what I wished without worrying about Lew's daily assessment of what I had done and how I had managed things while he was at work. I devised for myself tedious projects that would fill my time while Lew was gone, so that I would not be tempted to reflect on my life or to give breath or hope to the few remaining visions of another life that still existed somewhere deep inside of me.

The day after Lew left, I was mending one of Lew's shirts when Hildy called for me to come downstairs. At first, I thought perhaps Arianne had somehow learned that Lew would be gone and had come to visit. This thought filled me with both warmth and dread. As I descended the stairs, I noticed that the visitor was not Arianne, but a young man who appeared to be Lew's age. He was handsome, although in an entirely different way than Lew. Whereas Lew had striking ebony hair and a slender, toned figure, this man was broad shouldered and stocky with chestnut curls and silver green eyes that seemed magnetic in their intensity. Some feeling that I could not identify settled in me. When I reached the bottom of the stairs, the man smiled, and I was captivated. He held out his hand as he said, "Ah, you must be Blodeuwedd."

"I am sorry, do I know you?" I asked, uncertain.

"No. But I have heard great things about you. I am here to see Lew."

"I'm sorry," I replied, disappointed though I knew not why. "Lew is out of town this week."

"I knew I should have called ahead, but I wanted to surprise him. I'm Mr. Fox, Brian Fox, a good friend of Lew's. Lew and I roomed together in college and had a good many adventures together. Lew had sent me an invitation to your wedding but unfortunately I had not updated him on my whereabouts so the information did not get to me in time. In fact, I just recently found out that he had pledged his life to the most beautiful woman for miles around. I knew that I would be in the area, and I just had to see my old friend and this woman of great legend."

I pulled a somber face and said, "Well, sir, you have just sealed my Lew's fate. I had no idea that the man I love was betrothed to another woman!"

Confused, Brian stuttered, "I'm—er-sorry, I..."

"You said that Lew was pledged to the most beautiful woman for miles around. Have you seen the women in these parts, Mr. Fox?"

"Brian, please, call me Brian."

"Very well, Brian. As I was saying, this town is quite well known for its bounty of beautiful women. Surely, I can't be the most beautiful of them all!"

A sly smile crept across his face, and I knew immediately that I liked this man.

"Well, Blodeuwedd, I don't disagree that there are likely many beautiful women in this area, but surely their beauty pales next to yours. Besides, I have never known Lew to settle for anything less than the best. In any case, Mrs. Mathowny, I suppose I should be on my way. There is just one problem."

"What is that?" I asked, perplexed.

"Lew and I had a longstanding bet. I had a bit of a reputation in school for being a romantic and I shamefully admit a weakness for love. In my younger, more immature years, I was always pledging my undying love to some woman or another. Lew was convinced that I would be the first of us to wed but I knew that I was far too fickle for that prophesy to come true. Lew had quite a way with the ladies himself and so I bet him that he would be the first to settle down, once the right woman caught his eye. So, we did what men do, we placed a bet—of a rather substantial sum I might say. Of course, I have matured a great deal since those days, as I am sure Lew has as well, but a bet is a bet and I wouldn't dare risk offending my old friend by not collecting on our bet. I would return to my home, but I am ashamed to admit that I was foolishly anticipating to collect my money which would sustain me until my next paycheck arrives. Alas, it looks like this was not meant to be and I do not want to burden you, so I will take my leave. It was a pleasure meeting you, Blodeuwedd."

"Mr. Fox—Brian—I am sure Lew would not want his good friend to be left without sufficient resources for lodging. I insist that you stay here until you get your check. We have a guest room and it would be no problem to get it ready for you."

"Blodeuwedd, surely I couldn't impose on you."

"I insist. Hildy will have your room ready in no time. In the meantime, can I get you something to eat or drink?"

"I assure you I will be no trouble. You won't even know I am here! I really do appreciate this, Blodeuwedd. A woman who is beautiful and kind! Lew is a lucky man! I am not hungry but I would love a tour of the house and gardens if you have time."

I spent the next few hours in Brian's company, and was amazed at how easy it was to talk with him and how interested he seemed to be in what I had to say. At first, I made a valiant attempt to refrain from interjecting my views but Brian had this innate ability to put me at ease and soon it felt remarkably natural to let my guard down with him. Brian was a writer, and very good at painting the most vivid pictures with his words. We talked about art and he was excited to learn that I had painted in my younger years. I could not understand how this man, who was so different than my husband, could have possibly been his best friend. I was surprised when I looked out the window and noticed that the sky was darkening. We both retired to our rooms, and I found myself looking forward to spending more time with this man.

The next day was spent taking Brian around town and talking more about our respective backgrounds. The weather was nice, so we had dinner together out on the balcony. I was enjoying the simple pleasure of being in this man's presence. As we were talking, I suddenly noticed a shooting star streaming across the sky.

"Oh!" I exclaimed in excitement.

"What is it? What's wrong?" Brian asked, concerned.

"Nothing's wrong. It's just that I saw a shooting star!"

"The stars are so beautiful on nights like this. Look, you can see the constellation of Orion right over there."

"And Andromeda! I didn't realize you were—"

"An amateur astronomer? Oh yes, I used to spend hours looking at the night sky, tracing the constellations with my fingers and imagining what it must be like up there. Part of my romantic nature, I guess. You should really get a telescope so that you can see the stars in more detail. Not many people take the time to look at such things, let alone comprehend how amazing and expansive and beautiful our world is. Not many people, but you…"

He broke off and his eyes met mine, and I felt my stomach turn as though I were standing on the edge of a cliff, looking down. I was more scared and more excited than I had ever been. I had no desire to betray my husband, and I wanted so desperately to tear myself away from him, but I couldn't seem to move. He leaned forward and his lips brushed mine. This, I thought, this is what I always thought love was supposed to feel like. Oh, why couldn't it be like this with Lew? With the realization of what I had done, I abruptly excused myself and ran to my room where I cried myself to sleep.

The next morning, I worked diligently to avoid Brian. I became enraptured with any task I could find that would take me away from his proximity. Finally, towards the end of the day, he caught up with me. I tried to leave, to make an excuse, but Brian grabbed a hold of my arm.

"Blodeuwedd, stop trying to avoid me! Would you listen to me for one minute? I wanted to tell you I'm sorry. I should never have kissed you last night and I assure you it was as much of a surprise to me as it was to you."

"Brian, I know you meant no harm and I do not bear you any ill will. I am sorry as well. I think it would be best though if—"

"I am not done, Blodeuwedd. I am sorry I put you in an awkward position. I always fancied myself to be a gentleman but a true gentleman would never have done that. I should leave the premises right now in an effort to spare you this discomfort and to retain any vestiges of integrity I have left. But… I can't. I have never met anyone like you. I can't stop thinking about you. I know it sounds crazy, Blodeuwedd, but I have never felt this way about anyone. I think…I think I am falling in love with you. I am so torn! Lew is a dear, dear friend and I don't want to hurt him but I can't help thinking he doesn't deserve you. I know that if you are honest with yourself, Blodeuwedd, you know that he doesn't make you happy. What would it take for us to live our lives together? What would it take to make you mine?"

For a moment, I felt I must be imagining this. Surely this couldn't be happening! This type of love, this proclamation of desire only happened in fairy tales. I felt loyal to Lew and in my head I knew that I was not strong enough to leave him, to bring disgrace upon him in this way. But Brian's speech had awakened something in me that I had thought was gone forever and my heart overruled my head as I rushed into his arms and allowed myself to be swept away.

Attempting to cram a lifetime's worth of memories and shared revelations into a mere few days, we spent every moment together that we could. We tried to be discreet, to perpetuate the image of platonic acquaintance whenever others were around, yet we looked for opportunities to escape the watchful eyes of others whenever possible. This was somewhat easy to do, except when it came to Hildy.

Throughout the time that I had been married to Lew, Hildy and I had grown close. She knew me too well to be fooled by my attempts at normalcy. Hildy's loyalty to me as well as her unique relationship as both my friend and confidante and a household employee deterred her from confronting me directly. One day, as she was helping me to get ready to go out, Hildy subtly insinuated that perhaps Lew and Brian weren't as close as Brian had asserted.

"Oh?" I asked. My curiosity had gotten the best of me but I was trying to remain aloof. "Why do you say that?"

"As I recall, he and Mr. Mathowny had a rather substantial falling out—over a young woman, I believe. Mr. Fox can be quite charming, Blodeuwedd, but I wouldn't believe everything he tells you. Just be careful, my dear."

I started to ask her what she meant, but the look on her face made it clear that she was unwilling to say anymore. I confronted Brian about the love triangle Hildy had implied had occurred. Brian admitted that he had been smitten with a girl—Elizabeth—and had dated her only to have her stolen away by Lew, but he assured me that they were young and immature when this happened and that they were always a bit competitive. Brian said that he and Lew fought briefly but couldn't stay mad at each other for very long. When I asked him what became of the girl, he laughed and said that she and Lew did not last very long and he doubted if Lew even remembered her name. His easy acknowledgement and explanation of the situation reassured me and assuaged any feelings of doubt that had been planted in me by Hildy's comments.

The day before Brian left, we talked about what hope we had for our future. Brian wanted desperately to tell Lew, and to free me from what had become a loveless marriage. I so wanted to begin my life with Brian without delay, but I could not bear to think of hurting Lew and having him feel that he had, once again, been abandoned by a woman that he loved.

Lew returned from his trip and I worked especially hard making sure his needs were met and acting the part of the loving, dutiful wife so as not to give him any reason to doubt me. I informed Lew nonchalantly that Brian had stopped by to see him, and Lew seemed genuinely happy at the mention of his old friend. This, of course, caused my feelings of guilt and despair to embed themselves even deeper in my heart. I had no reason to be concerned that Lew would suspect anything, however, as he was absorbed in his work and just as distant and unaware of my feelings as ever.

Lew was required to travel twice more in the weeks that came and Brian and I planned clandestine rendezvous each time. Most of our time together was filled with stimulating conversation and passion. I found that Brian was very much a dreamer, and while I admired this trait in him, I feared that perhaps his confidence in our ability to bring the vision of our lives together to fruition was not based in reality. Brian readily admitted that he had never settled for long in one place. I wondered whether his wanderlust was born of a desire to keep his life interesting and adventurous or out of an inability and unwillingness to form commitments and work through challenges when they occurred. On the eve of our last night together before Lew was due to return back from his most recent trip, Brian and I argued about Lew and although Brian finally agreed to give me more time to decide how and when to end things with Lew, I wasn't altogether sure that I could trust his word.

My guilt was further compounded when Lew returned home. Having heard through the grapevine that he was positioned for a career promotion, Lew's father boasted to anyone who would listen about his son's success. Lew beamed with pride when he told me this, and in a rare jubilant and loving mood, he pulled me to him and began kissing me with a hungry look in his eyes. To be honest, I was not expecting his reaction and what could I do other than to give in? I certainly couldn't tell him that I was in love with another man and would be leaving him soon. Once again, I fell back into the role that my parents and Lew had created for me and which I had become so accustomed to during our marriage.

When I first began to feel ill in the mornings, I was worried that something was wrong with me and that this would interfere with my ability to fulfill my obligations according to Lew's standards. I thought that perhaps the stress of my affair with Brian and my unhappiness with Lew had brought about the decline in my health. Hildy recognized the changes in my body and my appetite and my frequent trips to the bathroom in the morning. I tried hard to act as if nothing was wrong. Hildy approached me one day and asked if I was alright. I confessed that I was not feeling well and asked her not to tell Lew.

"Hildy, please don't say anything. I swear I will see the doctor if I am not better by next week," I avowed.

"Better? My dear, it's going to take more than a week for you to feel differently." Perplexed, I asked, "Why is that?"

Hildy gave me a puzzled look and said, "Most women don't feel 'better' for nine months. Blodeuwedd, don't you realize? You are pregnant, my dear."

As soon as she said the words, I knew they were true even though I desperately wished they weren't. I tried blocking them out, tried living in denial, but there was no doubt that I had a child growing inside me—and no idea which of the men I cared for was her father. I knew I could not hide this from Lew or Brian for very long. I begged Hildy not to say anything, and she assented. I needed time to figure out what I was going to do.

Meanwhile, Lew's hard work had paid off. He had won his case and was being promoted to the position of full partner within the law practice he worked for. He was ecstatic and thrilled when the local newspaper published an article about his success. The Mathowny family was well known in the area, so it was not surprising when the story spread to neighboring towns and the law practice began getting phone calls inquiring about the promising young lawyer who was poised to become the youngest full fledged partner the law firm had ever seen. Lew's employer planned an extraordinary gala in Lew's honor to be attended by all of his friends and family and to welcome him as a full partner in the firm.

The day before the gala was to be held, I heard a knock at the door, followed by Lew's shouts of joy. I tentatively made my way down the stairs, and came face-to-face with Brian.

4

"Why, it's been years, friend! What brings you to my humble abode?" Lew clapped a hand on Brian's back in a jovial manner.

"It seems I missed you the last time I was in town. Besides, I was in the area and I couldn't just let the chance to spend time with the most celebrated young lawyer in the region slip by me, now could I? Blodeuwedd," Brian addressed me with a more formal tone. "It is good to see you again. In honor of your hospitality during my previous visit, I brought you a small token of my appreciation."

I wasn't sure what to think but I couldn't risk arousing suspicion or concern in Lew, so I hesitantly began opening the package handed to me by Brian and cried out in delight when I saw its contents.

"It's a telescope! Oh, Brian—I mean—Mr. Fox—this is beautiful, but I really can't accept this."

"Please," Brian replied, "You must. As I said, it's just a small token of appreciation for making me feel so at ease when I arrived unannounced last month."

Lew shook his head, laughing, and said, "You are too much, Brian! Why, who else but a rogue like you would think to give such an impractical gift? Still the dreamer, are you?"

Brian just smiled and I politely thanked him before heading off to find Hildy to let her know that we would be entertaining a guest. I did not say much the remainder of the evening, but simply watched as Lew and Brian reminisced about their college years. It seemed as though Lew was enjoying catching up with Brian, but I could sense that Lew's good natured ribbing that must have been a hallmark of their friendship was causing some subtle yet powerful tension. I told both men that I would be retiring for the evening, yet once I was sure that Lew was asleep and the house was still, I quietly made my way to the guest room to confront Brian.

"What are you doing here?" I demanded.

"What, are you not happy to see me?"

"I am always happy to see you, but I don't understand why you are here. You show up unexpectedly, give me a present that you know will have great meaning to me, and for what? You could have jeopardized everything that we have been planning for. What if Lew suspected—"

"Lew is a fool!" Brian whispered harshly. "An arrogant fool who is too self absorbed to take notice of anything or anyone else. Besides, Blodeuwedd, we cannot put it off forever. We must tell him! Continually putting it off only prolongs the pain. We have no choice…that is, unless you have changed your mind about us…"

"No, of course not!" I avowed. I wanted so desperately to tell him about the baby. We had talked about having children and I knew he would be excited at the prospect of being a father. For some reason I couldn't explain, I could not bring myself to tell him anymore than I could bring myself to be honest with Lew.

"Alright, perhaps you are right. I know that we need to tell him, it's just… tomorrow night is so important to Lew, to his career. His friends and family will all be there. Can't we just wait a little bit longer? Doesn't he deserve to be happy for just one more night?"

"I don't get it, Blodeuwedd. He isn't concerned about your happiness, yet you have sacrificed and would continue to prolong your misery to ensure that he is happy? Do you truly love me, Blodeuwedd? Are you truly willing to sacrifice his happiness for our love, our freedom? Are you really strong enough to fight for what you want?"

"Yes!" I cried defensively. Though I myself had pondered these very same questions on more than one occasion, I was shocked and hurt that the man I loved would doubt me as well. "I will tell him. Just give me one more day. Promise me that—promise me you will let me wait until after Lew has had his moment in the spotlight."

Brian begrudgingly agreed to give me more time, and we silently clung to each other for a brief time before I slipped out of his arms and walked back to my room. The remainder of that night, I had disturbing dreams. I was being chased by not one, but two predators and despite running as fast as I could through a maze of trees in the thick of the night, I could feel the predators' breath on my neck. Just as it seemed I was about to be devoured by one or both of the predators, I transformed into an owl and flew away and awoke in a cold sweat.

The next morning, it seemed as though any resentment Brian had felt towards his friend had faded. Lew and Brian were inseparable, and Lew insisted that Brian attend his gala. For some reason that I could not name, I felt a strange foreboding that Brian's attendance at the event would end in certain disaster. There was nothing I could do to prevent this from happening as there was no way for me to talk with Brian alone. And how could I explain to Lew that his dear friend should not be at his side for such an important moment in his life? The event was everything it had promised to be and more. In addition to Lew's colleagues and our immediately family and close friends, the gala was attended by a veritable who's who of high society. I once again played the role of the proud wife to perfection, despite the emotional turmoil I felt.

Lew continued in his teasing, competitive banter with Brian and though he did not seem to notice it, I sensed that Brian was becoming increasingly resentful. Brian joked with Lew and appeared to laugh off Lew's jibes, but I could see Brian's smile starting to fade. I excused myself from the room when the toasts started, as I was feeling a bit nauseous. After taking some time to splash cold water on my face and rest for a bit, I emerged from the bathroom to hear Lew introducing Brian and boasting that perhaps someday Brian, too, would have a stellar career, financial success, and a beautiful wife. It was at that moment that Brian asked to lead a toast in honor of his friend. I was overcome by an ominous dread and I shrank back from the room, torn between my desire to run and my need to hear what Brian would say.

"To Lew," Brian began, holding his drink in the air and enchanting the crowd with his charming smile. "I have known this man for quite some time now, much to my chagrin." The crowd laughed at Brian's jest. "You look at Lew, and might think, 'This man has it all! A great career, a strong family reputation, a gorgeous house, wealth beyond the imagination of most, and perhaps of most importance to many of you bachelors in the audience, a beautiful, loving wife." Some of the men in the audience shouted, "Here, here!" and they all raised their glasses to toast, but Brian silenced them.

"Alas! There is much you may not know about the man we are honoring tonight. Did you know that in the 3rd grade, this rogue got in trouble for kissing a girl and making her cry? Yes, he was a ladies' man even then! Unless, of course, you were making that up, my friend."

Appreciative laughter filled the room, and Brian continued. "But I believe it. Did you know that this scoundrel stole my one true love in college? Elizabeth was her name. I pledged my undying love for her and my friend swept her up from under my nose only to break her heart irreparably a mere few months later." At this, the room was silent, and Brian's face was somber and pained. Just as the silence became awkward, Brian recovered and a sly smile returned to his face. "Scandalous, I tell you! Of course, we had quite a row and by the time we were done, we were both so bloodied and ugly that no girl would look at either of us for weeks!"

At this, the audience laughed in a way that was part appreciation and part relief.

"Obviously, Lew recovered his good looks and despite the skeletons I have uncovered for you all, this man still shines bright. He still appears to have it all! But Lew, I would bet that there are still a few things that you don't know, a few surprises yet in store, if you will."

Still believing that Brian's speech was all in good natured fun, Lew cried out, "What's that, Brian? Are you going to tell me that you have inherited a fortune? Better yet, have you once again met a beautiful girl—the envy of all men unlike some of these other dogs you have pledged your love to in the past—and finally decided to settle down? That, my friend, would be shocking!" Lew guffawed as he brought his glass to his lips.

No, no, NO! I thought. I could see what was coming next, but I could do nothing to stop it.

"As a matter of fact, dear Lew, I have. I came here to not only honor you but to introduce you to the woman who has captured my heart, the woman who has shown me the true meaning of love and passion, a woman whose beauty puts all other women to shame. I would like to introduce you to her, but I can't. I can't Lew because—"

"Because she doesn't exist!" shouted Lew, and the room once again erupted in laughter.

Waiting for the last strains of chuckles to die out, Brian paused, still smiling, and said, "No, Lew, you can't meet her, because you already know her. The woman who I am madly in love, the woman who I have spent hour upon stolen hour of paradise with, is your wife."

I heard the hush come over the room and saw as Lew's smile froze on his face right before I ran from the room. I heard Lew scream at Brian and the sounds of a scuffle. Tears streaming down my face, I ran as fast as I could in the direction of our home. It was a lie, I thought. Brian didn't truly love me anymore than Lew did, I was a pawn. I knew that at some level Brian cared deeply for me, but obviously his need for vengeance overrode any feelings he might have had for me. How could I have been so blind? How could I have let myself be so swept away? I walked through the door of my house to find Hildy standing there, and I collapsed at her feet sobbing.

Hildy led me to the sitting room and between sobs I told her the entire story. "What am I going to do, Hildy? I can't face Lew and there's no point in facing Brian. I can't go to my parents, not after I have smeared their reputation and destroyed everything that they have done for me, everything they have done to further our family? I have no one and nowhere to go!"

"Hush, dear, you must think about the baby."

Somehow, caught up in the storm of my emotions, I had forgotten about the baby. Now, I felt a surge of love, strength, and protectiveness that had previously felt outside of my reach. I knew that anything I had had with Brian was over. I knew without a doubt that I could not allow Lew to raise my child. What was more, I knew that I wanted my daughter—for I felt certain that I would bear a daughter—to have the strength and opportunity to govern herself and forge her own way and to live a life that she chose, rather than one chosen for her. That would never happen if Lew were to raise her. Despair gripped me and terror coursed through me as I recalled Hildy's tragic revelations surrounding Arianne's decision to leave her husband.

Hysterical, I clung to Hildy, pleading, "Hildy, I can't let them know that I am with child! I can't risk having my daughter torn from me. I don't know what to do! I have to leave but how can I? There is no place to go, no one who can help me!"

"There is one person who may be able to help, child," Hildy somberly responded.

"Arianne."

Hildy helped me as I rushed to pack a few treasured possessions, including the necklace my father had given me and the telescope that had been Brian's gift. I gazed briefly at the wedding ring that had symbolized my commitment to Lew and though it was meaningless now, I was compelled to keep it for my child to have someday. I knew I had to hurry, for there was no telling what was happening at Lew's event and at some point, someone—most likely Lew— would come looking for me. Arianne greeted me at the door with a loving embrace and asked, "Are you sure this is what you want? If you leave now, there is no looking back."

Choking on my sobs, I felt weak, unable to move. What made me think that I was strong enough to take this step, when I had never been able to do so before? Immediately, the answer came to me. Love. Not the one dimensional love that I had thought I had felt for Lew, for Brian, even for my parents. But a love more powerful than anything I had ever experienced. A love for my unborn child, and despite everything that had happened, a newfound love for myself. My voice was steadier than it had ever been, as I answered, unequivocally, "Yes".

Much of the initial part of my journey with Arianne was silent as I was overcome with thoughts, questions, and emotions. Arianne vowed that she would find a way to keep Hildy apprised of my well being just as Hildy had kept her apprised of Lew's well being as a child. Although I never asked Arianne where she was taking me, it was not long before I figured out where we were going. Glastonbury. The knowledge filled me with a longing, excitement, and trepidation. I began asking Arianne about the women and the community there, and what it meant to train as a priestess. Arianne answered my questions patiently and as she did, I felt the fear melt away and endless possibilities arise. At first, I thought only of the opportunities and freedom my daughter would have and the strength and self-love she was bound to experience being raised amongst a community of independent, loving, supportive women. I almost wept with joy when I realized that I would be able to pursue my passions of art and astronomy unrestrained. The whisper of promise at learning the old ways stirred a remembrance in my soul.

As our boat neared the island, the mists enshrouded us, but Arianne skillfully navigated us through the heavy tendrils of fog to the bank of the island. She held my hand and looked intently at me. And though we were silent, we needed no words to convey the feelings and emotions that threatened to overtake us.

As we crossed the threshold that would lead us away from the mist and into the island's light, I felt the essence of my potential and all of the possibilities that had been kept afloat within me by the barest flicker of hope stir and come to life—and I was reborn.

Epilogue

My years on the island transformed me. As I prepared for your birth, I began the process of rebirth myself. As I guided your growth from child to woman, I, too, undertook this journey, albeit in a different way. It was as if I had been in a cocoon in my previous life in the mundane world and the turmoil preceding my departure had been the catalyst for the chrysalis to burst open and free me from the last remains of fear, guilt, and doubt so that my transformation was finally complete. I rediscovered my love of art, and spent many an evening with my telescope learning about the constellations and the effects of the stars on our destinies. I was thrilled when Arianne asked me to teach some of the younger girls in these areas as well. I learned the knowledge of our ancestors and used this knowledge to heal the most fragile parts of myself, to discover and reclaim my inner power, and to emerge from the ashes of my past a stronger woman, a nurturing mother, and a priestess in every sense of the word. All of this, while running after a beautiful, fiery, vibrant little girl who I had named Yarrow!

I suppose you wonder why I chose that name. I remember you giving me grief about it sometimes, wanting to know why I couldn't have named you something "beautiful" like Morgan or Raven. When I was little, before my mother prevented me from romping through the countryside, I would stare in fascination at the yarrow, with their spindly little leaves and their delicate white flowers. I found it remarkable that something that was so beautiful and appeared so delicate could be so sturdy and strong, thriving in areas where other flowers could not survive. I had quite forgotten about this flower until I was learning about herb lore shortly after I arrived here in Glastonbury. For weeks, I had been trying to figure out what to name you, but nothing felt right. When I was reminded of the yarrow, something just clicked. When I learned that the leaves of the yarrow were said to be effective in halting bleeding, I almost whooped with joy! For you, little one, were destined to be both beautiful and strong and your existence was the most powerful force in halting the waves of grief that threatened to overcome me when I would remember all that I had lost, all that I—and those that I had cared for—had endured.

Although I have never spoken with anyone from my past—other than Hildy—I have heard about their lives from time to time. When Lew returned home that evening, demanding to see me, Hildy told him that I had returned home briefly, gathered a few of my things, and left without a word. She insisted that she tried to find out what was wrong, tried to stop me, but that I wouldn't listen. Fortunately for Hildy, Lew believed her.

My father never quite recovered both from losing me and from the shock and disgrace he and my family suffered as a result of my actions. Hildy sent word that my father passed away suddenly shortly after my departure. My mother was quite distraught. To Lew's credit, he allowed Hildy to stay with my mother and look after her for a time after my father's death. Lew was devastated over my betrayal—though whether he was more pained by the loss of his wife or the damage my indiscretions did to his family's reputation, I cannot be sure. He and Brian had come to blows that fateful night, and for a time he attempted to drown his pain in alcohol. Fortunately, his father stepped in and helped him to rebuild his career and his life. I had heard that Lew moved to another town and remarried a young woman from a well to do family. I do not know much more than that. As for Brian, I had heard that after realizing the implications of what he had done and upon hearing that I had disappeared without a trace, he fell apart. He apparently looked for me for quite some time, but to no avail. The last I heard, he was travelling from town to town, trying to eke out an existence.

Although much of my story has focused on the reasons for the choices I made and the betrayals I experienced with both Lew and Brian, my intent is not to paint either man in a bad light for I believe that they both cared for me in their own way and perhaps even to the extent that they were capable. They, too, were reacting to the pain that they had experienced in their own lives and the influences which formed their beliefs and views. Though I don't know which man was your father, I see elements of each of them in you. Like Lew, you are resilient, determined, hard working, and charismatic. Like Brian, you are gifted with a vivid imagination and boundless creativity, you paint worlds with your words, and you can charm the pants off of anyone you meet!

I hope that my story, my lessons will serve you well as you make your way in this world, dearest child. I know that you are both scared and excited at the prospect of blazing your own trail and experiencing all that life has to offer. At times, you may feel as though your efforts are futile, or as though you are not worthy of the love and happiness that are within your reach. Know this, my child, you are stronger and wiser than you could ever imagine. As you have no doubt learned during your short life on this island, the goddess exists within each and every one of us and who could possibly deny the worth of a goddess? To believe that you are not good enough, not smart enough, not worthy enough is to do an injustice to Her.

The path will not always be easy, and you will no doubt have to bear some pain and sacrifice along the way. Promise that you will be true to yourself; that you will treat yourself with all of the love and warmth that you have shined upon countless others. Know this—I will always, always be here for you, ready to offer my guidance, support, and unconditional love.

Brightest blessings and love,
Blodeuwedd

BLODEUWEDD

by Virginia Bowman

Night Prayer to Blodeuwedd

BY JULIE BOND

O Blodeuwedd,
Maid of flowers, the Oak, the Broom, and the Meadowsweet;
Lady called forth by Math and Gwydion,
I greet you this night.
In the darkness, Flower-Face, your eyes see deeply, your
talons grip tightly.
Help me to see deeply into the darkness of confusion;
To hold fast to my true path as it leads me onward.
O Blodeuwedd, Flower-Face,
O Lady who made your own choice;
As blossoms garland the land and all Nature blooms forth,
I honour you this night and this Spring.

Blodeuwedd: Regaining One's Own Power

BY FRANCES BILLINGHURST

When one of the leading poets of the 14th century, Welshman Dafydd ap Gwilym (c1320-c1380), penned his poem "Chwedl Blodeuwedd" ("A Shriek of Blodeuwedd"), little did he know that centuries later it would inspire the likes of Robert Graves[1] (author of *The White Goddess: A Historical Grammar of Poetic Myth*) and more particularly, Alan Garner's 1967 teenage fantasy novel *The Owl Service*.[2] This was because the poem had allegedly been rejected by the Canon of Parry on the grounds that Dafydd had already written a poem to an owl.

The inspiration of the Blodeuwedd character mentioned in Dafydd's poem is found within the latter part of the "Fourth Branch" of the *Mabinogion*,[3] in the story of "Math ap Mathonwy ("Math the son of Mathonwy"). Math was considered to be the most powerful magician in northern Wales and ruled the area known as Gwynedd. When he had to replace his foot-holder, his niece, Arianhrod (daughter of the Goddess Don), was convinced by her brother, the magician Gwydion, to apply for this position. One requirement was that the foot-holder had to be a virgin; so when challenged whether she was, Arianhrod responded: "I do not know but that I am".[4] As she stepped over Math's magic wand, however,

---

[1] Graves, Robert, *The White Goddess: A Historical Grammar of Poetic Myth* (Farrar Straus Giroux, 1997).

[2] Garner, Alan, *The Owl Service* (Collins, 1967).

[3] A 19th century translation of two earlier manuscripts (the *Red Book of Hergest* and the *White Book of Rhydderch*) compiled by Lady Charlotte Guest, that contained eleven stories, four of which, the "Four Branches", are believed to have been written around the 11th century.

[4] Gantz, Jeffrey (translated), *The Mabinogion* (Penguin Books, 1976).

Arianrhod "dropped a fine boy child with rich yellow hair"[5] named Dylan (who disappeared into the sea), and shortly after another bundle that, before anyone else had noticed, Gwydion wrapped up in a sheet of silk and placed inside a chest in his room. This bundle became the fair haired Lleu Llaw Gyffes ("fair one with a skilful hand").

Humiliated and angered by these events, when Gwydion later brought the child before Arianhrod to acknowledge, she placed three *tynghedau*[6] upon the child:

1. Only she could name the child;
2. Only she could provide him with arms;
3. He would never have a wife who was human.

Through acts of cunning and trickery, Gwydion successfully overcame the first two *tynghedau*. The third, however, required the assistance of Math's powerful magic. With his assistance, Gwydion was able to create the "fairest and most beautiful maiden anyone has ever seen"[7] out of three sacred flowers,[8] being oak, broom and meadowsweet. This non-human and somewhat shadowy character they called Blodeuwedd ("flower face").

The three plants chosen for the construction of Blodeuwedd each have a long esoteric association within both druidic teachings of the Welsh, as well as the later Anglo-Saxons. The oak is renowned as being held sacred to the druids, from which they took their name *derwo-weyd* (*derwo* meaning oak), as it was a tree that was known for its strength. Broom is known for its golden yellow flowers that appear in spring and summer from which yellow dye can be made. Despite a traditional Saxon rhyme stating that *"Sweep the house with blessed broom in May/sweep the head of the household away"*, sprays of the yellow broom flowers were a common form of decoration of wedding brooms. Finally, meadowsweet (also known as "Lady of the Meadow" and "Meadow Queen" amongst other names), was popular in the making of wine and beer, as well as having a number of medicinal properties.

In "Math ap Mathonwy", shortly after his marriage to Blodeuwedd and having

---

[5] Jones, Gwyn, and Jones, Thomas (translation), *The Mabinogion* (Dragon's Dream, 1974).

[6] Plural of the word *tynged* meaning a prohibition that is usually determined by fate.

[7] Gantz, Jeffrey (translated), *The Mabinogion* (Penguin Books, 1976).

[8] In his poetic work *The White Goddess*, Robert Graves mentions that Blodeuwedd is created from nine sacred plants, these being primrose, bean, broom, meadowsweet, cockle (burdock), nettle, oak, hawthorn and chestnut.

been given the uplands of Ardudwy in a distant part of Wales, Lleu decided to visit his uncle Gwydion, leaving his new bride alone in their castle. This decision eventually turned fatal for Lleu. During his absence, Blodeuwedd witnessed a hunter in the nearby woods. Through a seemingly innocent act of hospitality, she offered food and lodgings to the hunter, who was the dark haired lord of Penllyn, Gronw Bebyr. However, the pair fell in love with each other, and realized that the only way they could be together was if Lleu was killed.

Knowing that he was half divine, Blodeuwedd was also aware that Lleu could only be killed in a specific way. Under the pretense that she was afraid for his safety, Blodeuwedd begged her husband to inform her how this could be achieved so that she could prevent such situations from occurring. Lleu, not suspecting anything malicious from her, advised that the only way he could be killed was during a time that was neither day nor night, at a place that was neither indoors nor outdoors, when he was neither riding nor walking, and was neither clothed nor naked. The only weapon that could actually kill him was a spear that had taken a year to make.[9] In other words, Lleu advised his wife that he could only be killed at dusk, wrapped in a net, with one foot on a cauldron and the other on a goat, and by a spear forged for a year during the hours when everyone was at church. Armed with this information, Blodeuwedd commenced preparation for her husband's death by instructing Gronw how to make the spear.

A year later Blodeuwedd questioned her husband again about the circumstances by which he could be killed. This time, however, she asked that Lleu demonstrate how this could be done. Again, not expecting anything untoward from his wife, he did just this, only to be struck down by a spear thrown by Gronw who had been hiding close by.

The spear hit Lleu in the thigh (or groin) and instead of being killed outright, the wounded Lleu was transformed into an eagle that flew away. This allowed Gronw to rule both Penllyn as well as Ardudwy now.

When Gwydion became aware of the situation, he went in search of his nephew. During this time, he came across a farmer whose sow would vanish during the day and no one knew where she went as they could not keep up with her. When she returned in the evening however, she was very well fed. Gwydion decided to follow the sow and discovered that she was feasting on the rotting flesh of

---

[9] Jones, Gwyn, and Jones, Thomas (translation), *The Mabinogion* (Dragon's Dream, 1974).

an eagle that was perched in the tree. Realising that the eagle was in fact Lleu, Gwydion sang the following *englyn* (a traditional Welsh poem) that brought the eagle closer to him so that he was able to return Lleu to human form:

Cymraeg/Welsh	Saesneg/English
Derwen a dyf rhwng dau lyn	Oak that grows between two lakes;
yn cysgodi'n dawel awyr a glyn	Darkening gently sky and glen
oni ddywedaf i gelwydd	Unless I tell a lie,
o flodau Lleu y mae hyn.	From the flowers of Lleu are these.
Derwen a dyf mewn maes uchel	Oak that grows in upland ground,
nis gwlych glaw, nis tawdd gwres	Rain wets it not, heat burns it not
cynhaliodd ugain dawn	It contained twenty gifts
ar ei brig Lleu Llaw Gyffes.	It bears in its branches Lleu of the Skilful Hand.
Derwen a dyf dan lechwedd	Oak that grows beneath the slope
noddfa tywysog hardd	Shelter of a fair prince
oni ddywedaf i gelwydd	Unless I tell a lie
fe ddaw Lleu i'm harffed.	Lleu will come to my lap.

After being nursed back to health, Lleu sought to reclaim his lands that Blodeuwedd and Gronw had claimed in his absence. When confronted by the man he thought he had killed, and realizing that the outcome of this battle would result in his own death, Gronw pleaded that since he acted through the "wiles of a woman,"[10] he should be allowed to place a stone between himself and the blow. Lleu granted this boon. However, when he threw his spear, it pierced both the stone and Gronw, killing him outright. Meantime, Gwydion tracked down Blodeuwedd and turned her into an owl as a form of eternal punishment for her adultery and treachery after advising her that:

> "You will not dare to show your face ever again in the light of day ever again, and that will be because of enmity between you and all other birds. It will be in their nature to harass you and despise you wherever they find you. And you will not lose your name - that will always be 'Bloddeuwedd.'"[11]

The story of "Math ap Mathonwy" concludes with Lleu eventually gaining the throne of Gwynedd.

The initial perception of Blodeuwedd is that of an unfaithful wife and traitor,

---

[10] "Blodeuwedd" by Anna Franklin (http://www.merciangathering.com/blodeuwedd.htm).

[11] Parker, Will, *The Four Branches of the Mabinogi* (Bardic Press, 2007).

however as Australian Celtic artist and author Lynne Sinclair-Woods[12] points out, Blodeuwedd is what can be described as a "flower bride;" that is, a woman who lives her life by following the rather emotional ideals of romantic love, which are usually detrimental to her own sacred role (usually being the "embodiment of the essence of life and its relatedness with the land and all life."[13]) Other examples of such women include Branwen (who also appears in an early story found within the *Mabinogion*), Guinevere (from the Arthurian legends), and even to some extent, the late Princess Diana (until her divorce).

Sinclair-Wood further believes that women acting as "flower brides" tend to cast themselves as emotional and weak women who need to be "saved" by a more powerful man.[14] In Blodeuwedd's case, being created by men for a man, she initially appeared to be the perfect woman – dependent and submissive. It is only during her husband's absence and through the meeting of Gronw Bebyr that Blodeuwedd begins to regain her "whole self;" that is, becoming in touch with the true power of the feminine. When this occurs, she awakens to the realization that there is more to life than living solely for her husband.[15] Little wonder, this realization is met with much resistance from Gwydion and Lleu.

Living as "flower brides," is an action that ultimately leads to either the destruction of the women themselves and their lovers; or on the other hand, in the women finding themselves transformed to higher awareness (the owl that Blodeuwedd was turned into is often associated with wisdom). When they eventually become true to their own selves and start demonstrating their own will and desires, "flower brides" are often seen as "upsetting" things.[16]

The lover of the "flower bride" is usually a man without awareness of his connection with the feminine as the "Principle of Life" (something to be found within him through the guidance of self-realized women). Instead he chooses to see the feminine as a projection upon a living woman, who reflects his idea of what a woman should be, rather than the reality of the whole woman.[17]

There is another element to the story of Blodeuwedd, which is her being the "Sovereign Goddess of the land with whom the sacred king must marry in

---

[12] Sinclair Wood, Lynne, *Creating Form from the Mists: The Wisdom of Women in Celtic Myth and Culture* (Capall Bann, 2001).
[13] Ibid.
[14] Ibid.
[15] Ibid.
[16] Ibid.
[17] Ibid.

order to rule."[18] Blodeuwedd is created out of spring flowers, is betrothed to Lleu at summer and according to author Anna Franklin, buried at the early autumn festival of Lughnasadh.[19] This makes Blodeuwedd the central focus around which the age-old seasonal battle occurs, that of the light and dark kings battling for the hand of the Goddess. In this story, Lleu is the light or solar king and Gronw, the dark king. As in a similar fashion to the British folkloric battle of the Oak and Holly King who meet each solstice to battle for the hand of the Goddess, the timing of the battle between Lleu and Gronw is at each equinox.[20]

Associated with change and transformation, Blodeuwedd reminds us of the realization of our own potential, which can only be obtained by our own selves and not through others. She also reminds us that while we are uniquely individual, we are ultimately all connected in the greater scheme of things in that when we change and transform, others are affected (even on a minute level), opening the door for their own transformation as well. For example, Lleu, who is also created by Gwydion, is transformed through Blodeuwedd's actions. As such, Blodeuwedd is more than a traitorous wife—she is the much needed catalyst for Lleu to discover his true and authentic self.

A Shriek of Blodeuwedd ("Chwedl Blodeuwedd")
by Dafydd ap Gwilym (paraphrased by Giles Watson)

White owl, Welsh ghost,
Pale wraith, a whole host
Hears your sharp shriek,
Thin fledgeling: hooked beak,
Barely feathered gosling breast,
Frail as a foundling beast,
Cleft-faced, elf-shot,
Yawning a blood-clot.

Sanctuary – tall tree!
Shrink away, leave me
Bearing the curse of Don,
Wrath of birds and Gwydion:
Short day, long night,

---

[18] "Blodeuwedd" by Anna Franklin (http://www.merciangathering.com/blodeuwedd.htm).
[19] Ibid.
[20] Ibid.

Crisp cold, grim plight.
Hide in hole, fleeing light,
Bird-mobbed, taking flight."
"What name, which word
Plagues you, grim bird?"

"Fine girl, great fame
Blodeuwedd my name,
Borne of proud Meirchion,
Love-child of great Mon."

"Princess? Words strange!
What man wrought the change?"

Gwydion at Conwy's tower
Lifted wand, made me cower,
Tore me from my delight:
Exiled to black night,
Once noble, now spurned,
Lust-bitten, love-burned.
By Gronw Pebyr, fair, foul.
Pale girl: frightened owl.

SOURCES

Gantz, Jeffrey (translated), *The Mabinogion* (Penguin Books), 1976.

Garner, Alan, *The Owl Service* (Collins), 1967.

Graves, Robert, *The White Goddess: A Historical Grammar of Poetic Myth* (Farrar Straus Giroux), 1997.

Jones, Gwyn, and Jones, Thomas (translation), *The Mabinogion* (Dragon's Dream), 1974.

Parker, Will, *The Four Branches of the Mabinogi* (Bardic Press), 2007.

Sinclair Wood, Lynne, *Creating Form from the Mists: The Wisdom of Women in Celtic Myth and Culture* (Capall Bann), 2001.

Song of Flowers (Cân y Blodeu)

BY TIFFANY LAZIC
With gratitude for the generous Welsh linguistic guidance of Kristoffer Hughes, Anglesey Druid Order

Oh Blodeuwedd prydferthwch annibynnol,
(Beautifully independent Blodeuwedd)
Duwies o rhith y blodeu,
(Goddess formed of flowers)
Anwylyd mewn dewis a ddim,
(Beloved in choice and not)
Bendigaid by' dy greadigaeth persawrus,
(Blessed be your fragrant creation)
Bendigaid by' tyfaint dy ymwybodaeth,
(Blessed be your growing awareness)
Bendigaid by' arwaith dy lais,
(Blessed be your voice in action)
Bid hŵt dolefus
(May the mournful hoot)
dy dylluan,
(Of your Owl)
Dyfod symudiadau doeth i'r Hun.
(Bring wise movement towards Self).

The Feast of Blodeuwedd

BY KATE BRUNNER

While studying with the Avalonian Thealogical Seminary and reading the work of Alexei Kondratiev, I begin pursuing the many aspects of food and their role in the Celtic Archetype. In particular, I spent a great deal of time combing through and meditating on his writings concerning the Tribe-Land connection. I devoted a significant chunk of time considering its importance to the Celts, but also how it has manifested throughout human history right up through modern day. I believe food to be THE primary physical manifestation of the Tribe-Land connection. What we physically consume is a tangible piece of the energy of the Land it was grown on and in. It is the portion of the Land, the body of the Tribe ingests into their very flesh. I am already a proponent of eating as local as possible and of connecting directly with the land one lives on, so this devotional project takes that passionate exploration further and explores new facets of it for me. Exploring Celtic diet, food production and preparation, and meal-related ritual allows me to further examine the Tribe-Land connection of our Avalonian foremothers. Cooking is an alchemical, spiritual practice at my own hearth. Food has great wisdom and great healing power when healthful connections are made to it. Learning how to create and apply food as spiritual nourishment seems to me to absolutely be the purview of a Priestess.

While diving into this personal study, I decided to create Feast Day menus for each of our Ladies of Avalon. The process allowed me to add a third branch to the Tribe-Land connection; that of Deity. Creating, assembling, preparing, and consuming a devotional meal—a Feast of the Goddess—produces a delicious ritual context for strengthening the bonds between Tribe, Land, and Goddess. I relied heavily on correspondences that came out of my research, readings, and intuitive workings. Then, I combined the flavors the best I could with what foods I felt corresponded the strongly with each Lady. Not every ingredient 100% corresponds. For example, the butter in an entrée might not be specifically a food I would necessarily correspond to a specific Goddess' feast. But the core ingredient and the method of cooking may balance that out by being specific correspondences for me. Ingredients and cooking methods represent my blending of Celtic foods/dishes, modern foods corresponded to a particular Lady, and the culinary influence of Australia—the Land where I currently live. Most of the ingredients used are foods available in Canada and the US, as well.

Ritually, these meals would be appropriate for a Lady's arrival or departure through the Avalonian Cycle of Healing or any other time in which one wishes to embody Her, welcome Her energies into oneself, honor Her or otherwise connect with Her via the Fruits of the Land. The Goddess Feasts are all five course meals in keeping with the importance of the five-fold structure to our Tradition. The soup is served before the main and the salad after which is more commonly European, but also simply my personal preference.

Blodeuwedd's feast is a sensuous meal. It is the bread broken between the Goddess of the Land and her chosen Sovereign. It is to be eaten with one's fingers, fed to each other between whispers and caresses. To join Blodeuwedd at Her table is to surrender to Her love, to allow yourself to woo and be wooed.

Entrée: Steamed Baby Artichokes with Lemon Butter Dipping Sauce

This is actually a dish from my childhood. My mother used to make this for our six member family using full sized artichokes as a rare treat for dinner. Those dinners are actually a very fond, very loving, very sensory-filled memory for me. We each got our own artichoke and then shared bowls of dipping sauce between every couple of us. An artichoke is actually a flower blossom! We would pull each individual petal off one at a time, dip it through the salty, buttery, lemony sauce and scrape the slightly bitter meat off the inside of the petal with our top teeth, tossing the leaves in a communal bowl when we were done with them. Around and around we went, pulling each layer of the artichoke blossom apart, eating each petal, hands and chins greasy, with smiles and joyful chatter all around. When all the leaves were gone, we got down to the choke. Each of us, in our own time, scraped the heart clean of the layers of prickles with a small spoon. Then, ladling the last of the sauce into the chalice of the heart, we nibbled every last morsel of that up, too. It is a sensuous dish, to be savored with eyes, hands, nose and tongue. And it shouldn't be eaten alone.

Soup: Nettle Soup with Spring Onions

Every relationship needs to be kept healthy, to be nurtured. Sometimes we come up against something prickly and we have to work to transmute it into something more nourishing. Nettle, an herb linked to Blodeuwedd in our Tradition, carries this as one of its many lessons. You can use a basic potato soup base and add fresh nettle leaves at the end of the cooking process. Stirring them into the hot soup until they are just wilted will neutralize their sting, but retain their best nutritional components. Spring onions should be used as a garnish just before serving.

Main: Honey-Spiced Quail (or Cornish Hen/Poussin) on a Bed of Baby Vegetables

Another dish that despite its sophistication, demands to be eaten with one's hands. How else will you be able to enjoy every last morsel? The roast fowl is meant to correspond with the avian nature of the Owl Maiden. The honey is a reminder of Her time as Flower Bride, source of nectar. The mixed spices represent the additional flavors Her transformation manifested in Her being. Experiment with what savory spices bring out new aspects of your culinary personality—cardamom, cinnamon, star anise, nutmeg, paprika, and more. Let your senses guide you. Smell them, taste them, mix them together in a spoonful of honey and see what inspires you. Don't forget to experiment with different honeys, as well. Robust, dark honeys keep good company with spice. Once you've discovered your perfect mixture, massage your bird with the honey-spice blend, inside and out, before roasting. Don't forget to baste liberally. Serve the roast bird on top of your steamed baby vegetables. The juices from Blodeuwedd's sweetness and spice will blend and co-mingle through the bed of vegetables, bringing their flavors to lightly steamed carrots, sugar snap peas, pearl onions and patty pan squash, or whatever other veggies you've chosen. These are the first spring hints of the larger, more robust harvest to come.

Salad: Spring Herb Salad with Asparagus Tips, Chevre, & Chive Vinaigrette

Designed to refresh you after a heady main course, this should be a salad of mostly spring greens and assorted green herbs, such as parsley, coriander, thyme, tarragon or whatever else is seasonally available and appeals to you. Top the greens and herbs with lightly broiled asparagus, dot with chevre (goat cheese) and toss with a slightly tangy, but simple dressing. A dressing of olive oil, vinegar, chopped chives and salt and pepper would be perfect.

Dessert: Fruit & Flower Pavlova

A pavlova is an antipodean dish. Australians and New Zealanders like to argue about who invented it first. It consists of a large baked meringue base topped with fresh whipped cream and an assortment of seasonal fruits. You just need a basic meringue recipe, but instead of piping it into small pieces, you bake it as one large circle until the crust just barely begins to brown. Allow the base to cool first before spreading a layer of fresh whipped cream over it. I prefer to use cream I've whipped myself with no added sugar. The sweetness of the base plus the fruit is enough for me. For Blodeuwedd's pavlova, strawberries, blueberries, or any other spring berries share the seasonal spotlight with edible flowers in honor of the Flower Bride—rose petals, violets, or red clover blossoms would all be good possibilities.

I encourage you to use this Feast of Blodeuwedd as a starting point. While you can certainly just use this menu, the power of the ritual would be strengthened greatly by spending time designing your own personalized feast. You can do this through a combination of study and experience. Examine each Lady's mythology for references to food, feasting, farming, etc. I also recommend researching Celtic materials discussing food and food-related customs from ancient to modern times via historical record, mythology, and folk tradition. Spend time in sacred space exploring food-based connections to each Lady and the Station of Cycle She governs. Combine these internal and external observations into a unique devotional meal of your own!

Emergence

BY JHENAH TELYNDRU

The last whisper of owl's wings
Feather dawn's tendrils
Over the softening horizon,
Curling like mists
Over the conquered darkness
Of the waning night.

Slumbering buds awaken—
Aroused into fragrant bloom
By morning's sweet kiss.
How like the spring, my soul!
Seeking the light
And, touching it,
Opening into full beauty.

© 2002

OAK OF THE WHITE SPRING

by Kate Brunner

Flying with Blodeuwedd

BY CHRISTINA MCCLENDON

Breath deepens
In and out.
Lungs expand
In and out.
Eyelids close and the waves appear.
As the wave crests, I see Her face.
And then She is gone.

Another wave comes, again, Her face.
The curve of Her smile, the wisps of hair under Her hood,
The wide large eyes of Blodeuwedd.

Stillness.
Complete Bliss.
Perfect Unconditional Love.

Come with me,
Fly with me,
See through my eyes…

We wind our way into the tree trunk and up the spiral staircase.
At the top, the staircase opens to one lone branch.
We walk out together.

What is your heart's desire, my love?
Our eyes meet and we smile with complete understanding.

My arms open and the feathers spring from my skin.
My eyes widen, and where my feet once stood, now talons,
sharp and ready.
With a deep breath and complete confidence, I take flight and
soar through the moonlit night.

The apple orchard is so small from this height!
The Tor approaches, and we circle our ancient and Sacred Space.
Silver leaves glisten on the trees in the dark of night.
The water around the island ripples and sparkles with the movement of the cool night wind.
Above us, the stars are glittering orbs of light, illuminating our flight.

What do you see, my love?
Her soothing voice sings in my mind.
I search for the "right" answer in the underbrush of the trees, the apple that has fallen to the ground, or maybe the budding plant near the Tor.

No, my love. What do you SEE?
Colors, auras, and a patchwork of light appears all around me and my eyes fill with love and beauty.

What do you hear, my love?
Again, I strain to find the detail she seeks.
The insect's beating wings? The rattle of the leaves in the wind? The rippling song of the water below?

No, my love. What do you HEAR?
A soft symphony tickles my ears and the song grows as I soar in the night.
A host of animals, plants, and insects perform the sweetest love song I have ever heard.

What do you feel, my love?
I spread my wings and spread my talons.
This time, I am sure I understand.
The wind. The mist in the air. The cool temperature on the surface of my body.

No, my love. What do you feel?
My heart and lungs fill with warmth that spreads to the tips of my wings and into my belly and through my feet.
It is the caress of Wholeness, Authenticity, and Oneness.

We soar back to the tree and as we float to the ground, the transformation begins again.
My toes touch the cool grass and my eyes adjust to the full moon above.

What did you learn, my love?
There are no words.
We embrace, and the beauty, the symphony, and the warmth of her touch
pervade every cell.
With tears in my eyes, I understand.
I have tasted pure freedom.

The drum beats and the return is bitter sweet.
The breath deepens again.
My toes and fingers move, sweeping into a curved stretch and a slight yawn.
Eyelids softly blink as the knowing smile spreads across my lips.

Until we fly again, Blodeuwedd.

5/7/2014

You Will Fly

Blodeuwedd

Christy Croft

Words and Music by Christy Croft © 2015 All rights reserved.

as you soar. And so you make your plans to free your heart and free your hands and for a time your life is yours 'til Gro-nw's fall and Gwy-di-on's re - venge. 3.Fea - thered queen of sov - ereign - ty, bound no lon - ger will you be. Ex tend your wings, spread them wide, the world be - fore you lies. You will fly, you will fly through the night, through the sky. Fear and doubt are left be - hind as you soar.

Words and Music by Christy Croft © 2015 All rights reserved.

2

An Invitation...

We sincerely hope you have enjoyed this volume, dearest reader. It is our intention to not only share with you our collective devotion to Blodeuwedd, but also to inspire you towards deepening your own relationship with our beloved Flower Face.

To that end, we place here nine fresh pages ready for you to use. As your relationship with the Owl Maiden blossoms and flourishes, we hope these pages will invite you to continue to grow this body of devotional work and make it your own.

May the blessings of Awen be with you. /|\

185

Contributors

Laura Bell

Laura is an Artist and Illustrator from the UK. She is inspired by nature, animals and all things mystical! To see more of her work please visit: www.mymysticalart.blogspot.co.uk

Frances Billinghurst

Frances Billinghurst is a prolific writer with an interest in folklore, mythology, and ancient cultures. Her articles have appeared in various publications including Llewellyn's *Witch's Calendar, The Cauldron, Unto Herself: A Devotional Anthology to Independent Goddesses, A Mantle of Stars: A Devotional to the Queen of Heaven, Naming the Goddess,* and *The Faerie Queens.* She is the author of *Dancing the Sacred Wheel: A Journey through the Southern Sabbats,* and *In Her Sacred Name: Writings on the Divine Feminine* and the editor of *Call of the God: An Anthology Exploring the Divine Masculine within Modern Paganism.* When she is not writing, Frances is attempting to replicate the Hanging Gardens of Babylon on her patch of Australian dirt, and journeying between the worlds. More information about Frances can be found through her writer's blog (http://francesbillinghurst.blogspot.com.au).

Julie Bond

Julie comes from Liverpool and grew up on the North-West coast of England. She has been working in the Druid Tradition for over twenty years and has studied with the Order of Bards, Ovates, and Druids (OBOD) as well as being a member of the Sisterhood of Avalon (SOA) since 2007. She now works mainly with the Order of the Sacred Nemeton (OSN), a Druid monastic order.

Tammi Boudreau

A therapist, priestess, and Sister, Tammi was a long time member of the Sisterhood of Avalon before she journeyed to the Holy Isle in 2004 after a two year battle with breast cancer. She served in leadership as a member of the SOA's Council of Nine, and took an active role in the administration of the Avalonian Thealogical Seminary. It was her wish that the chants she wrote as a reflection of her devotion to the work of the Avalonian Tradition continued to be shared with women after her passing, and so it is with deep love that we include Tammi's work in this anthology.

Virginia Bowman

Virginia began her path following a God and Goddess polytheism path in 1999. After many years of joining different spiritual groups, attending various pagan events, and researching many different paths, she has embraced her ancestral Scottish roots and joined the Sisterhood of Avalon in 2010. She resides in Ontario, Canada with her best furbaby Gabriel and embraces local natural environments for inspiration and channels that raw energy into her creative paintings. You can contact her by e-mail: videobyv@email.com

Emily Brunner

Emily Brunner is an artist and designer whose work often deals with mythology, magic, dreams and the surreal. She holds a Bachelor's degree in fine arts and an Associates degree in graphic design. Her work has been featured in drawing publications and she has done work for the Sisterhood of Avalon. Visit her at: www.emilybrunner.com.

Kate Brunner

Kate Brunner is a writer, healer, ritualist, & member of The Sisterhood of Avalon, studying at the Avalonian Thealogical Seminary. She is a somewhat nomadic American, homeschooling her children with the world as their classroom. She holds a BA from Tulane University, where she studied Economics, International Relations, & Religious Traditions. Kate is a presenter at Red Tents, Goddess conferences, & women's spirituality retreats. She also hosts seasonal women's gatherings, facilitates labyrinth rituals, and leads workshops on an assortment of women's spirituality topics. Her written work on women's spirituality appears in two Moon Books anthologies, *Paganism 101: An Introduction to Paganism by 101 Pagans* and the forthcoming *Goddess in America*. Kate is also a Project Co-Weaver at the Feminism and Religion Blog Project, where she works as a contributor, editor, & technical coordinator. She currently serves as Hearthkeeper Matron on the Council of Nine. You can read more of her work at: http://feminismandreligion.com/author/katembrunner/.

Adara Bryn

Adara Bryn is a singer of songs and teller of tales, and is an enthusiastic believer of bare feet on the ground and in using one's voice. She has been transplanted in the green lands of Georgia, where she lives with her three children, husband, two cats of varying attitudes, and one loyal and spirited Golden. For twenty-some years her passions have included traditional music, myth, folklore, and Women's Mysteries. She was a member of the Sisterhood of Avalon from 1999-2016, and has served as Lorekeeper Matron on the Council of Nine and as Director of the Avalonian Thealogical Seminary.

Robin R. Corak

Whimsical yet complex, Robin Corak is an unpredictable funhouse with a knack for introspection and a relentless determination to explore the world around her and go after what she really wants with empathy and love. A member of the Sisterhood of Avalon since 2002, Robin's work has been featured in publications and sites including the *Sisterhood of Avalon 2014 Datebook*, PWP's *Yule Anthology* (2012), and *The Tor Stone*. Robin and her endless imagination reside in Washington State with her husband, son, stepson, two dogs and one cat who thinks he's god....but what cat doesn't?
Visit her at www.peacelovemischief.com.

Christy Croft

Christy Croft is a graduate student in the humanities and social sciences with a strong interest in Celtic mythology. An avid singer and musician, she lives in rural North Carolina with her partner and five children. A sampling of her spiritual writings can be found at www.thesacredloom.com.

Sharon Crowell-Davis

Goddess first spoke to SharonLynn in the 1950's when she was a little girl exploring the woods of Oak Ridge, Tennessee, formerly known as Site X, home of the Manhattan Project. Through years of walking a convoluted path she became a veterinarian, earned a PhD with a focus in Neurobiology and Behavior from Cornell University, and experienced the mystery of 'Riding Between the Worlds' on her horses. While in veterinary school in the 1970's, she read Evangeline Walton's books that are a modern interpretation of The Mabinogion, and echoes of those stories have clarified and guided her further walking the path of serving Goddess ever since. She joined the Sisterhood of